OCR SHP GCSE

CRIME & PUNISHMENT

c.1250 TO PRESENT

Pranav Rajasekar W4

JAMIE BYROM
MICHAEL RILEY

DYNAMIC LEARNING

HODDER
EDUCATION
AN HACHETTE UK COMPANY

The Schools History Project

Set up in 1972 to bring new life to history for school students, the Schools History Project has been based at Leeds Trinity University since 1978. SHP continues to play an innovatory role in history education based on its six principles:

- Making history meaningful for young people
- Engaging in historical enquiry
- Developing broad and deep knowledge
- Studying the historic environment
- Promoting diversity and inclusion
- Supporting rigorous and enjoyable learning

These principles are embedded in the resources which SHP produces in partnership with Hodder Education to support history at Key Stage 3, GCSE (SHP OCR B) and A level. The Schools History Project contributes to national debate about school history. It strives to challenge, support and inspire teachers through its published resources, conferences and website: **http://www.schoolshistoryproject.org.uk**

This resource is endorsed by OCR for use with specification *OCR Level 1/2 GCSE (9–1) in History B (Schools History Project) (J411).* In order to gain OCR endorsement, this resource has undergone an independent quality check. Any references to assessment and/or assessment preparation are the publisher's interpretation of the specification requirements and are not endorsed by OCR. OCR recommends that a range of teaching and learning resources are used in preparing learners for assessment. OCR has not paid for the production of this resource, nor does OCR receive any royalties from its sale. For more information about the endorsement process, please visit the OCR website, www.ocr.org.uk.

The publishers thank OCR for permission to use specimen exam questions on pages 104–105 from OCR's GCSE (9–1) History B (Schools History Project) © OCR 2016. OCR have neither seen nor commented upon any model answers or exam guidance related to these questions.

Every effort has been made to trace all copyright holders, but if any have been inadvertently overlooked, the Publishers will be pleased to make the necessary arrangements at the first opportunity.

The wording and sentence structure of some written sources have been adapted and simplified to make them accessible to all pupils while faithfully preserving the sense of the original.

Hachette UK's policy is to use papers that are natural, renewable and recyclable products and made from wood grown in sustainable forests. The logging and manufacturing processes are expected to conform to the environmental regulations of the country of origin.

Orders: please contact Bookpoint Ltd, 130 Park Drive, Milton Park, Abingdon, Oxon OX14 4SE. Telephone: (44) 01235 827720. Fax: (44) 01235 400454. Email: education@bookpoint.co.uk. Lines are open from 9 a.m. to 5 p.m., Monday to Saturday, with a 24-hour message answering service. You can also order through our website: www.hoddereducation.co.uk

ISBN: 978 1 4718 6011 9

© Jamie Byrom, Michael Riley 2016

First published in 2016 by
Hodder Education,
An Hachette UK Company
Carmelite House
50 Victoria Embankment
London EC4Y 0DZ

www.hoddereducation.co.uk

Impression number   10 9 8 7 6 5 4 3 2

Year   2020 2019 2018 2017

Cover photo: Mary Evans Picture Library/Alamy Stock Photo

Typeset by White-Thomson Publishing LTD

Printed in India

A catalogue record for this title is available from the British Library.

CONTENTS

INTRODUCTION

Making the most of this book

● **Where this book fits into your GCSE history course**

The course

The GCSE history course you are following is made up of five different studies. These are shown in the table below. For each type of study you will follow one option. We have highlighted the option that this particular book helps you with.

OCR SHP GCSE B

Paper 1 1 ¾ hours	**British thematic study** ● The People's Health ● Crime and Punishment ● Migrants to Britain	**20%**
	British depth study ● The Norman Conquest ● The Elizabethans ● Britain in Peace and War	**20%**
Paper 2 1 hour	**History around us** ● Any site that meets the given criteria.	**20%**
Paper 3 1 ¾ hours	**World period study** ● Viking Expansion ● The Mughal Empire ● The Making of America	**20%**
	World depth study ● The First Crusade ● Aztecs and the Spanish Conquest ● Living under Nazi Rule	**20%**

The British thematic study

The British thematic study takes just one theme in British history and traces the way it has developed from about 1250 to the present day. The point of this type of study is to remind you of the characteristic features of life in Britain across all those centuries and to strengthen your understanding of how and why things change or, perhaps, stay the same.

As the table on page 4 shows, you will be examined on your knowledge and understanding of the British thematic study as part of Paper 1. You can find out more about that on pages 98 to 105 at the back of the book.

The chart below shows exactly what your examination specification requires for this thematic study.

Crime and punishment, c.1250 to present

The specification divides this thematic study into four periods:

Periods	Learners should study the following content:
Medieval Britain, c.1250–c.1500	• The characteristic features of medieval Britain: an overview • Crimes and criminals in medieval Britain • Enforcing law and order including policing and different types of court • Punishing offenders: capital punishment, fines, whipping, public humiliation and imprisonment
Early Modern Britain, c.1500–c.1750	• Major religious, political and social changes: an overview • The changing nature of crime including vagrancy, moral crime and witchcraft • Enforcing law and order including secular and church courts and the roles of different law enforcers • Changes in punishment including the introduction of the 'Bloody Code'
Industrial Britain, c.1750–c.1900	• The enlightenment, urbanisation and political change: an overview • Crimes and criminals in industrial Britain including the increase in crime in the first half of the nineteenth century • The introduction and development of the police force • Changes in punishment including the growth of prisons, transportation to Australia and prison reform
Britain since c.1900	• Major technological, social and political changes: an overview • Changes in the crime rate and in types of crime • Changes in law enforcement including the use of new technology • Changes in punishment including the abolition of capital punishment and changes in prisons

Issues and factors

The bullets in each period tackle similar **issues**:

● An overview of life in the period. This will not tell you directly about changes in health care, but it helps to explain the issues that follow.
● The nature and extent of crime.
● The enforcement of law and order.
● The punishment of offenders.

The specification also says you should be able to explain how each of five **factors** have affected crime and punishment:

1. Beliefs, attitudes and values
2. Wealth and poverty
3. Urbanisation
4. Government
5. Technology

The next two pages show how this book works.

3

How this book works

The rest of this book (from pages 8 to 97) is carefully arranged to match what the specification requires. It does this through the following features:

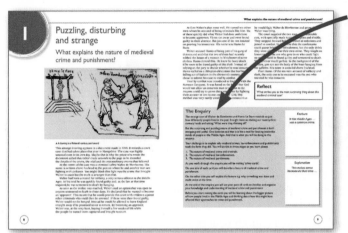

Enquiries

The book is largely taken up with four 'enquiries'. Each enquiry sets you a challenge in the form of an overarching question.

The first page or two of the enquiry sets up the challenge and gives you a clear sense of what you will need to do to work out your answer to the main question. You will find the instructions set out in 'The Enquiry' box, on a blue background, as in this example.

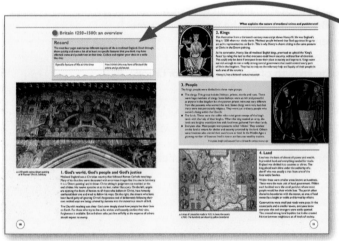

'Record' tasks

From that point, the enquiry is divided into four sections. These match the bullet points shown in the specification. You can tell when you are starting a new section as it will start with a large coloured heading. Throughout each section there are 'Record' tasks where you will be asked to record ideas and information that will help you make up your mind about the overarching enquiry question later on. You can see an example of these 'Record' tasks here.

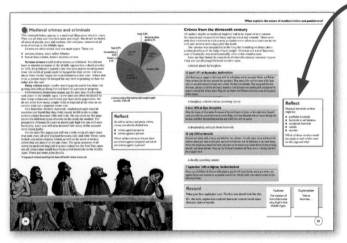

'Reflect' tasks

At regular intervals we will set a 'Reflect' task to prompt you to think carefully about what you are reading. They will look like the example shown here.

These 'Reflect' tasks help you to check that what you are reading is making sense and to see how it connects with what you have already learned. You do not need to write down the ideas that you think of when you 'reflect', but the ideas you get may help you when you reach the next 'Record' task.

'Review' tasks

Each enquiry ends by asking you to review what you have been learning and to use it to answer the overarching question in some way. Sometimes you simply answer that one question. Sometimes you will need to do two or three tasks that each tackle some aspect of the main question. The important point is that you should be able to use the ideas and evidence you have been building up through the enquiry to support your answer.

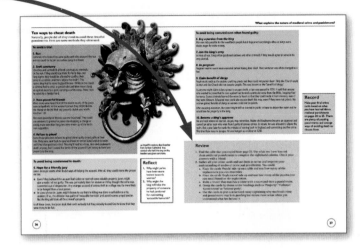

Closer looks

Between the enquiries you will find pages that provide a 'Closer look' at some aspect of the theme or period you are studying. These will often give you a chance to find out more about the issue you have just been studying in the previous enquiry although they may sometimes look ahead to the next enquiry.

We may not include any tasks within these 'Closer looks' but, as you read them, keep thinking of what they add to your knowledge and understanding. We think they add some intriguing insights.

One very important final point

We have chosen enquiry questions that should help you get to the really important issues at the heart of each period you study, but you need to remember that the examiners will almost certainly ask you different questions when you take your GCSE exam. Don't simply rely on the notes you made to answer the enquiry question we gave you. We give you advice on how to tackle the examination and the different sorts of question you will face on pages 98 to 105.

▲ An illustration from a fourteenth-century manuscript

These curious illustrations appear in the margins of a medieval manuscript from the late fourteenth century.

In the scene above, a fox has caught a goose and is running back to his lair. Although a woman chases him, he seems to have made a safe escape from the scene of his crime. But he hasn't.

The image on the right shows another illustration from the same manuscript. The fox has been caught and hanged by a very unusual collection of law enforcement officers!

If you look carefully you will see:

- two geese acting as police constables, standing on guard with a club and a bow and arrow
- another goose, wearing some sort of chain of office and a fine sword: he may be the judge
- a fourth goose who has flown high above the tree to set up the rope and noose
- a hen and cockerel tugging at the legs of the fox to make sure he dies
- a small duck, looking on with approval as justice is done.

and punishment

▲ An illustration from the same fourteenth-century manuscript

Many illustrations like these are found in the margins of medieval books. They often have nothing to do with what is written on the pages. The monks who made manuscripts were allowed to illustrate them more or less as they wished. Their drawings provide fascinating insights into many different aspects of medieval life ... including crime and punishment.

The fox and geese drawings are entertaining but they make a serious point: justice in the Middle Ages depended almost entirely on the community. Their only hope of protection against theft and violence was for all the people in a town or village to play their part. If they took no action they were all likely to become victims.

As time has passed, the work of catching and punishing criminals has increasingly been handed over to professionals. There have been great changes, but underneath it all, there are continuities too. That is what this book is about. We cannot promise any more geese catching foxes but there may be other surprises along the way.

Puzzling, disturbing and strange

What explains the nature of medieval crime and punishment?

▲ A drawing in a thirteenth-century court record

This strange drawing appears in a document made in 1249. It records a court case that had taken place that year in Hampshire. The case was highly unusual even in its own day. Maybe that is why the priest who wrote the document added this rather crude artwork to the page as he recorded the details of the crime, the trial and the extraordinary events that followed.

At the centre of the case was a criminal called Walter de Blowberme. His name is written above his head in the picture where he and another man are fighting with pickaxes. You might think this fight was the crime that brought Walter to court but the truth is stranger than that.

Walter had been arrested for robbery, a very serious offence in the Middle Ages. At his trial he was quickly found guilty and, as the law at that time required,he was sentenced to death by hanging.

As soon as the verdict was reached, Walter used an option that was open to anyone sentenced to death in those days. He declared that he wanted to become an 'approver'. This meant that he would provide the court with evidence against other criminals who could then be arrested. If these were then found guilty, Walter would not be hanged. Instead he would be allowed to leave England straight away if he promised never to return. By becoming an approver, Walter was, at the very least, buying himself a few weeks of life while the people he named were captured and brought to court.

At first Walter's plan went well. He named ten other men whom he accused of being criminals like him. Six of these quickly did what Walter had done and chose to become approvers. Three ran away and were found guilty in their absence. But just one of the ten insisted on proving his innocence. His name was Hamo Le Stare.

Walter accused Hamo of being part of his gang of thieves and said that the two of them had recently robbed the house of a woman in Winchester of some clothes. Hamo denied this. He knew he faced death if he were to be found guilty of this theft. Instead of relying on the jury to decide whether he was innocent, Hamo called on a 200-year-old custom that had been falling out of fashion in the thirteenth century: he chose to submit his case to trial by combat.

Trial by combat was introduced to England with the Norman Conquest. It was based on the belief that God would not allow an innocent man or woman to die. Anyone could try to prove their innocence by fighting their accuser in one to one combat. By 1250, this method was very rarely used but Hamo insisted that he would fight Walter de Blowberme and prove that Walter was lying.

The court supplied the two men, at considerable cost, with specially made tunics, weapons and shields. They stepped forward before a crowd of onlookers and joined in combat. In cases like this the combatants could pause briefly for refreshment, but the only drink they were allowed was their own urine. They fought on knowing that the one who gave in or who could fight no more would be found guilty and sentenced to death. The survivor would go free. In the background of the picture, you can see the body of the loser hanging from the gallows. His name is scrawled above his head.

Poor Hamo. Of the ten men accused of robbery and theft, the only one to be executed was the one who insisted he was innocent.

Reflect

What strikes you as the most surprising thing about this medieval criminal case?

The Enquiry

The strange case of Walter de Blowberme and Hamo Le Stare reminds us just how differently people lived in the past. It might leave us shaking our twenty-first-century heads and asking 'What were they thinking of?'

But the surprising and puzzling nature of medieval crime and punishment is both intriguing and useful. One historian said that it is like a tool for looking inside the minds of people in the Middle Ages. And that is what you will be doing in this enquiry.

Your challenge is to explain why medieval crimes, law enforcement and punishments took the form they did. You will do this in three stages as you learn about:

1. The nature of medieval crime and criminals.
2. The nature of medieval law enforcement.
3. The nature of medieval punishments.

As you work through the enquiry you will be making 'crime cards'.

On one side of each card you will describe a feature of medieval crime and punishment.

On the other side you will explain the feature e.g. why something was done and made sense at the time.

At the end of the enquiry you will use your pack of cards to develop and organise your knowledge and understanding of medieval crime and punishment.

Before you start making the cards you will be learning about the bigger picture of how people lived in the Middle Ages and thinking about how this might have affected their approaches to crime and punishment.

Feature

In the Middle Ages ... was a common crime.

Explanation

This makes sense because at that time ...

Record

The next four pages summarise different aspects of life in medieval England. Read through them quickly and make a list of at least six specific features that you think may have affected crime and punishment at that time. Collect and explain your ideas in a table like this:

Specific feature of life at this time	How I think this may have affected the crime and punishment

▲ A fifteenth-century Doom painting at St Thomas' Church, Salisbury

1. God's world, God's people and God's justice

Medieval England was a Christian country that followed Roman Catholic teachings. Many of its churches were decorated with enormous images like this one in Salisbury. It is a 'Doom painting' and it shows Christ sitting in judgement on humans at the end of time. His twelve apostles sit at his feet, rather like a jury. On the left, angels are opening the doors of heaven to all those who believe in Christ, have honestly confessed their sins and tried to follow his ways. On the right, the sinners who have been found guilty of ignoring Christ's forgiveness and of deliberately following their own wicked ways are being ushered by demons into the monstrous mouth of hell.

The Church's teaching was clear: God cares deeply about how people live their lives on Earth. For those who try to live as he wishes and honestly confess their sins, forgiveness is available. But evil-doers who just live selfishly at the expense of others should expect no mercy.

2. Kings

This illustration from a thirteenth-century manuscript shows Henry III. He was England's king in 1250 when our study starts. Medieval people believed that God appointed kings to act as his representatives on Earth. This is why Henry is shown sitting in the same posture as Christ in the Doom painting.

At his coronation, Henry, like all medieval English kings, promised to uphold the 'King's Peace' by ruling the land so that everyone could live in security, without fear of disorder. This could only be done if everyone knew their place in society and kept to it. Kings were not rich enough to run a really strong central government that could control every part of life in the kingdom. They had to rely on the voluntary help and loyalty of their people in each area of the country.

◀ Henry III, from a thirteenth-century manuscript

3. People

The king's people were divided into three main groups:

- The clergy. This group included bishops, priests, monks and nuns. There were huge numbers of clergy. Some bishops were as rich and powerful as anyone in the kingdom but the poorest priests were not very different from the peasants who worked the land. Some clergy were very holy but many were not particularly religious. They were just ordinary people who earned a living within the Church.
- The lords. These were the nobles who ruled great sweeps of the king's lands with the help of their knights. When the king needed an army, the lords and knights would join him with local men gathered from their lands.
- Everyone else. Most people were peasants called 'villeins'. They worked on the land in return for shelter and security provided by the lord. Others were freemen who owned their own house or land. In the Middle Ages a growing number of freemen lived in towns and became wealthy traders.

▶ A priest, knight and peasant from a thirteenth-century manuscript

4. Land

Land was the basis of almost all power and wealth. It provided food and everything needed for trade. England was divided into counties or shires. The king placed each shire under the authority of a sheriff who was usually a man from one of the local noble families.

Within these were smaller areas known as hundreds. These were the main unit of local government. Within each hundred were the small parishes where most people would live their whole lives. The parish often shared its boundaries with the manor, an area of land owned by a knight or noble and farmed by villeins.

Communities were small and roads were poor. In the countryside and in smaller towns, everyone knew everyone else and strangers were easily spotted. This created strong local loyalties but it also created friction between neighbours at all levels of society.

▲ A map of Lancashire made in 1611. It shows the county c.1500. The hundreds are shown by yellow boundaries

5. Food and famine

Farming was by far the most important work in medieval England. Villeins farmed many small strips of land scattered around the manor. Everything depended on the harvest and every bit of every strip mattered to a farming family. If the harvest failed for any reason, such as bad weather, there could be hunger or even famine. This would disrupt society, creating debt and desperation for food. There was a terrible series of harvests early in the fourteenth century and this led to a great famine between 1315 and 1321. When the Black Death struck England in 1348 it killed millions and caused more hunger as large areas of land went unfarmed. War could also disrupt farming.

▶ The lines of medieval farming strips in the landscape at Bressington, Derbyshire are still visible today

6. War and rebellion

The smooth running of society depended on each person or group showing loyalty and obedience to those above. For most of the Middle Ages this worked well enough but there were times when the system came under severe stress and even broke down.

- Powerful lords rebelled against the king in the thirteenth century.
- The Peasants Revolt shook the nation in 1381.
- The second half of the fifteenth century saw the Wars of the Roses, a series of struggles for the throne that drew lords, knights and peasants into civil war.
- Kings also waged wars against France and Scotland.

Medieval people, especially young men, were very familiar with bloodshed and violence.

▲ The scene after a battle in the Wars of the Roses, from a fifteenth-century manuscript

7. Tools and technology

Almost all work was done by hand in medieval England. People's days were spent working alongside each other with tools such as axes, hammers and spades. It was common to carry knives and strong wooden staves. Laws required adult men to keep weapons and armour ready for use should they be called to serve their lord or king in war or to deal with local difficulties.

There were, of course, no telephones, televisions, cameras or computers. Most people could not read or write. Communication was usually done by word of mouth and it was hard to share important information and to keep accurate records. Priests were highly literate. Some worked as clerks, the office workers of the Middle Ages. They produced the hand-written documents that historians use to find out about these times. Only in 1476 was England's first printing press set up in London.

The limitations of science and technology also limited medicine, transport and building.

▼ Cooks butchering meat, from a thirteenth-century manuscript

8. Homes and possessions

This artist's reconstruction gives some idea of how a reasonably wealthy peasant family might have lived. People did not go out to work or to school in the way that modern families do so there would usually be someone in or around the house. This changed at harvest time when the whole family would be in the fields busily gathering the crops that their lives depended on.

The house has a timber frame with walls made largely from hardened mud. The windows have no glass but there are simple wooden shutters. Even the homes of wealthier people in towns were made in a similar way.

Farming tools and the men's weapons may be in a simple outhouse. All the family's other belongings are shown here. They may have earned some cash in coins by selling ale, vegetables or eggs. This cash and any other valuables, including special clothing, would be locked inside in the large oak chest. The animals are probably their most valuable goods. For much of the year, they would be kept inside overnight.

In country villages, families like this would live side by side for generations. Villeins were not free to move. They had to keep working for the lord of the manor in return for being allowed to live in this house on the lord's land.

▶ An artist's reconstruction of a medieval peasant's home

9. Life and leisure

Medieval people went about their work and tried to live in as much comfort as they could, caring for each other like the couple here, settling down to share a simple meal. They are probably fairly wealthy townspeople. Those with money in medieval England gave to those in need as part of their Christian duty. Most schools and hospitals are now paid for by taxpayers' money but in the Middle Ages they depended on the gifts of individuals.

The pattern of life was largely set by the Church calendar. Sundays were days of rest as were the many feast days to honour Christian saints. This couple may be drinking wine but the most common drink of the time was ale, partly as the brewing process made it safer to drink than water. This was less strong than modern beers but drink could lead to high spirits and misbehaviour of all sorts.

Feast days were also times when villages and towns held special fairs and events like football games with very few rules and plenty of physical contact!

◀ A detail from an illustration in a fifteenth-century manuscript

13

Medieval crimes and criminals

The criminals below appear in a medieval illustration of a law court. They are all men and they look poor and rough. But do not be fooled: all sorts of people, men and women, rich and poor, committed all sorts of crimes in the Middle Ages.

Crimes are often sorted into two main types. These are

- serious crimes, often called felonies
- less serious crimes, known as petty crimes.

Serious crimes would lead to severe punishment. You did not have to murder someone in the Middle Ages to face a death penalty. In 1275, King Edward I passed a law that said anyone stealing more than 12d worth of goods could be hanged for their crime. 12d was about three weeks' wages for most labourers at that time. Before that time, a person might be hanged for any theft depending on how the judge saw the case.

Petty crimes might involve stealing goods worth less than 12d, getting into debt or doing limited harm to a person or property.

Unfortunately historians cannot say for sure how much crime took place in the Middle Ages. Crime rates are often measured by how many crimes are committed per head of the population. We do not know how many people lived in England at the time so we cannot work out a national crime rate.

One historian, Barbara Hanawalt, studied just eight English counties and found that they held around 16,000 trials to judge serious crimes between 1300 and 1348. The pie chart on this page shows the different types of crime in the trials she studied. The proportion of homicide cases is alarmingly high but you will soon learn why. Later you will also discover how many of the accused were found guilty.

On the next five pages you will see a wide range of court cases that took place all over England between 1250 and 1500. These cases include examples of petty crimes as well as the sorts of serious crime that are shown in the pie chart. The great majority of all crime in medieval England was non-violent but the first four cases are all crimes that would have been called homicide in the Middle Ages. There are some grim details.

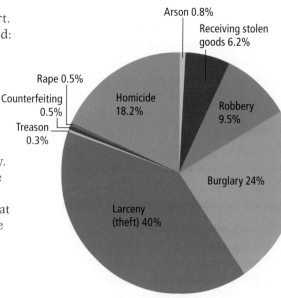
▲ Serious crimes that went to trial in eight English counties, 1300–48

Reflect

As well as serious and petty crimes, crimes can also be divided into

- crimes against property
- crimes against a person.

Which of the crimes in the pie chart are crimes against property and which are crimes against a person?

▼ A group of criminals awaiting trial, from a fifteenth-century manuscript

Crimes from the thirteenth century

All sudden deaths in medieval England had to be reported to a coroner. He viewed and measured the body and recorded any wounds. There were only four coroners in each county so bodies were often in a bad state by the time one arrived some days after the death.

The coroner was responsible to the king for recording evidence about sudden deaths with the help of local people. This was not a trial but every case of homicide was tried eventually, often a few months later.

Here are four homicide cases from thirteenth-century coroners' reports. They are not all straightforward murder cases.

A brutal attack by burglars:

23 April 1271 at Ravensden, Bedfordshire

John Reyd was at supper in his house with his wife Maud and his servants Walter and Richard. Felons entered by the door towards the courtyard. They struck John on the crown of his head with an axe and pierced his heart with a knife. He died immediately. They wounded Maud in the head, almost cut off her left hand, heated a trivet [a large iron cooking grill] and placed her upon it, leaving her almost dead. They tied up Walter and Richard and took away all the goods of the house.

A burglary, a death and an alarming injury:

4 June 1276 at Clun, Shropshire

Philip the Taylor of Clun broke the house of Reynold Kaym of Upton in the night-time; Reynold came out with his sword and tried to arrest Philip, who shot Reynold with an arrow through the testicles and fled. Reynold followed him and killed him with his sword.

A desperately sad case from Norwich:

25 July 1276 at Norwich

Richard was taken with a frenzy and killed his two children. His wife came home and found the children dead and cried out for grief, and tried to hold him, but he killed her in the same frenzy. When the neighbours heard the noise and came to the house they found Richard trying to hang himself, but prevented him. They say that Richard committed all these acts in a frenzy and that he is subject to it.

A deadly sporting contest:

7 September 1280 at Ulgham, Northumberland

Henry son of William de Ellinton while playing at ball with David le Keu and many others, ran against David and received an accidental wound from David's knife from which he died on the following Friday.

Reflect

Medieval homicide verdicts might be:

- justifiable homicide
- homicide in self defence
- accidental homicide
- suicide
- murder.

Which of these verdicts would you apply to each of the cases on this page and why?

Record

Make your first explanation card. The first side should look like this:

On the back, explain how medieval 'homicide' covered much more than just cases of murder.

Feature	Explanation
The number of homicides was very high in the Middle Ages.	This is because...

Crimes from the fourteenth century

Anger

Let's start this century as the last one ended, with another grim death:

6 November 1311 at Yelvertoft, Northamptonshire

William of Wellington, chaplain of Yelvertoft, sent a servant to John Cobbler's house to buy candles, but the same John would not send them without the money. For this reason the said William grew angry, took a stick, and went to the house of the said John and smote this John on the head so that his brains gushed forth and he died.

This is a straightforward case of murder – by an angry priest! Records suggest that over half of medieval homicides stemmed from simple arguments. The medieval system of strip farming meant that peasants had to work very close to each other and arguments were sure to occur just when sharp or heavy tools were at hand. To make matters worse, there was no effective medical care and wounds easily became infected. This also helps to explain the high homicide rate in medieval England.

Hunger

Arguments and thefts were worst at harvest times when the fields were full and the pressure was great. Crime also rose if a harvest failed and people found themselves in debt and in need. The first quarter of the fourteenth century saw a truly terrible run of harvests with famine across England in 1315–16. Maybe that explains some of these court cases recorded around those years:

1314 at West Halton, Lincolnshire

Thomas Amcotes says William Brotherstone owes him 25 shillings.

7 April 1316 at Birton, Yorkshire

The wife of Adam Shepherd of Heppeworth drew blood from Emma the wife of Adam Smith.

16 November 1316 at Wakefield, Yorkshire

Ellen, daughter of Richard Cosyn is accused of stealing two bushels of oats worth 12d from John Patrick's grange.
Eva, wife of William Cort, is accused of knowingly receiving the said two bushels.

1316 at Wakefield, Yorkshire

Hugh Skayfes accuses Robert Liftfast of the theft of one ox belonging to the said Hugh, the hide whereof was found in Robert's possession.

1320 at Barrington, Cambridgeshire

William, servant of John Marchant, took fishtraps and set them in private waters.

c.1321 at Chatteris, Cambridgeshire

John de la Haye ploughed on the land of the Lady Abbess of Chatteris, a furlong in length and two feet in width.

▼ Reasons for homicide, from medieval records 1300–48

	Number of murders	% of all murders
Argument	178	51.3
Domestic disputes	3	0.9
Revenge	2	0.6
Property disputes	13	3.7
Drinking	15	4.3
Self-defence	25	7.2
Jealousy	2	0.6
Accident	6	1.7
Robbery	85	24.5
Insanity	1	0.3
Others	17	4.9
Total	347	100

▼ Gathering the harvest, from the Luttrell Psalter, a collection of bible verses from the early fourteenth century

Reflect

How might bad harvests help to explain each of the court cases shown on this page?

▶ Graph showing the price of wheat and number of court cases for serious crimes in eight English counties, 1300–48. Court cases usually took place several weeks after the crime which explains the time gap between the two lines. Shillings were a type of currency used in Britain until 1971. There were 12 pence (d) in a shilling (s) and 20 shillings in a pound

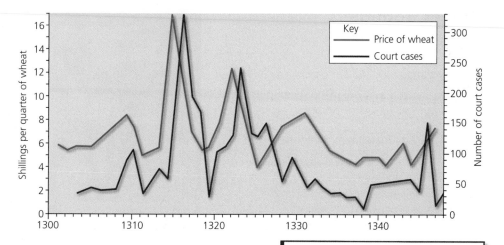

Suicide

This sad case shows another reason why the homicide rate was so high in the Middle Ages:

---

17 March 1343 at Oxford

(The coroner reports that) Henry de Bordesle died in the house of Richard le Coke. Henry had long been sick with diverse diseases and took a knife and smote himself in the belly for he was as it were mad. Afterwards he lived until the Sunday and then died of his wound.

Suicides were tried as cases of homicide in the courts. The Church taught that only God could decide when a person's life should end, so it was both a serious crime and a sin to murder yourself.

New crimes 1350–1400

In 1348, the Black Death struck Britain. Historians now believe that this plague killed 3.5 million people, which may have been over half the population. Society was severely disrupted, especially by the shortage of workers on the land. Cases of debt and theft were very common in the courts for a good number of years but in general terms the pattern of crime was very similar to the first half of the century.

As attitudes and circumstances change, new crimes appear. Here are two examples from this period. One just emerged from local court cases and the other came from a new law. They both went on to become serious issues in the early modern period (1500–1750).

Scolding was the use of offensive and abusive speech in public. Medieval manors were free to devise their own local laws and punishments. This one first appeared as a crime in some local courts after 1350. It then spread steadily. It was almost always applied to women, not men. Here is an example:

1359 at Bradford, Yorkshire

Three women are accused of being common and notorious scolds.

Vagrancy became a problem after the Black Death. There was a shortage of workers. Some left their manors and became vagrants, wandering the country trying to find work with better pay somewhere else. In 1351, Parliament passed a law that required all able-bodied men to swear that they would stay and work in their home village. In 1388, another law made it a crime for any labourer to leave their hundred without written permission.

Reflect

Which of the court cases on these two pages do you think are about serious crimes and which do you think are about petty crimes?

Record

Make some more crime cards. These could be about:

● why arguments might turn into murders so easily
● why crime went up at harvest time
● why suicide was treated as a crime of homicide
● why new laws could appear without an Act of Parliament
● why vagrancy became a crime in 1388.

Crimes from the fifteenth century

Outlaw gangs

The most feared and despised of medieval criminals were gangs of robbers:

▲ An ambush by robbers, from a thirteenth-century manuscript

---
2 April 1402 at Tottenham, Middlesex

Robert Berkworth alias Bekworth alias Edward the Hermit. Thomas Andrew alias Edward Kelsey, Thomas Draper, William Faunt, John Russell of Somerset, Richard Hauteyn and Alice Leche with other felons on the highway between Tottenham and London, lay in ambush and robbed two unknown men [i.e. strangers] of ten pounds of silver in money.

Throughout the Middle Ages, gangs like this ambushed travellers and robbed houses or threatened to burn them down if villagers did not hand over their valuables. They even killed shepherds just to take their clothing.

Many gang members were outlaws, on the run after being accused of committing crimes in their home village or town. England had great areas of forest where these outlaw gangs could live unchallenged. Any that were caught might even be given a pardon by the king if they promised to serve in his army overseas.

Bad behaviour and bad beliefs

Here is a crime at the other end of the scale from violent gangs:

1411 at Winchester

William Silver, a cook, is accused of gambling with dice.

From time to time laws were passed against dice, football and other games. The Church said they were sinful as they encouraged idleness. The laws were often ignored but the Church did take action against gambling for money as well as other 'moral crimes'. These ranged from shaving beards on Sundays to committing acts of homosexuality.

The Church also dealt with the crime of heresy or spreading false Christian beliefs. From the end of the fourteenth century a group called the Lollards challenged Roman Catholic teachings about God's forgiveness and demanded to be allowed to read the Bible in English.

---
5 February, 1413 at Leicester

John Belgrave of Leicester is a Lollard and a notorious speaker against the pope and his power … and that William Mably parchment maker, Nicholas Taylor of Leicester, Ralph Chapman, Roger Goldsmith and Lawrence Barbour of Leicester are common Lollards and holders of deviant opinions against the laws of the Holy Church.

The Church feared that people might go to hell if they were free to interpret Christ's teachings as they wished – but it also wanted to preserve its own wealth and power. Challenging the teachings of the Church became a serious issue after 1500.

> # Reflect
>
> 1. Why did some of the gang at Tottenham have more than one identity?
> 2. Why was it possible for outlaw gangs to carry weapons without being challenged?

▼ A dice thrower, from a fifteenth-century manuscript. X-rays show that medieval dice sometimes contained tiny amounts of mercury that controlled how each one fell

Treason – crimes against authority

Until 1351, the crime of treason had never been clearly defined. An Act of Parliament passed in that year changed this. It had some surprising features. Take this crime, for example:

> **9 September 1420 at Rothwell, Northamptonshire**
>
> Katherine Beeston, gentlewoman, and John Colle, farmer, did feloniously murder Thomas Beeston, husband of the said Katherine.

Under the 1351 Act, this was not just murder, it was treason. Everyone had to know their place: husbands were thought to be the head of the family just as kings were the heads of their kingdoms. So Katherine, who killed her husband, was a traitor as well as a murderer!

Counterfeiting coins was also treason, but the most serious examples of treason were plots to kill the king. Few were as strange as this one:

> **12 November 1427 at Westminster, London**
>
> John Parker confesses that he and William Billington, Elias Davy and William Felton planned to kill the king and his uncles with the help of a clerk [probably a priest] who through sorcery could drain the life out of whomsoever he wished to kill.

Lords and retainers – crimes that abused authority

The last years of the fifteenth century saw a dreadful crime wave. The culprits were the rich and powerful. Medieval kings always struggled to keep their nobles and knights under control. Many rich landowners built up private armies of armed servants called retainers. They used them in feuds against rival lords. The winners then ruled their local area by fear and favouritism and abused their power. They were like modern gangster leaders who take control of whole neighbourhoods.

During the Wars of the Roses between 1455 and 1485, the problem was worse than ever. Here is how some families in Cornwall complained to the king about crimes committed by a powerful knight:

> **1475 – A petition to the king from landowners in Cornwall**
>
> To the king our lord, we call unto your gracious remembrance diverse murders and robberies, ravishments of women, extortion, oppression, riot, unlawful assemblies, forced entries to property, and wrongful imprisonments done by Henry Bodrugan in the county of Cornwall.

The problem was that Bodrugan was a supporter of the king and even wore the Yorkist badge. The king made little effort to control Bodrugan. This problem of lords and retainers only ended after 1500.

Meanwhile, on a different scale, our last two cases remind us of the sorts of petty crime that went on throughout the medieval period:

> **1476 at London**
>
> Alice Deyntee is accused of selling corrupt and old butter not wholesome for man's body.

> **1477 at Great Burstead, Essex**
>
> Two men of Great Burstead left dung and other garbage in the main street of Billericay in front of the chapel.

Reflect

Why do you think counterfeiting (forging) coins was counted as treason?

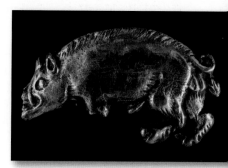

▲ A fifteenth-century retainer's badge. The boar was the emblem of Richard, Duke of York who became King Richard III

Record

Make some more crime cards. These could be about:

- why outlaw gangs could escape so easily
- why shaving a beard could land you in court
- why local lords could become leaders of organised crime.

Enforcing law and order

These two pages show who had the job of catching medieval criminals and who tried their cases in court.

The enforcers

The **king** was in overall charge of keeping 'The King's Peace'. In 1285, King Edward I passed the Statute of Winchester that tidied up many recent developments and shaped law enforcement in England for hundreds of years. This page shows a simplified version of how 'policing' was done from that time until the nineteenth century.

There was no full-time paid police force. That would have been far too expensive. Instead 'policing' was done on a voluntary basis. Everyone in society had to play their part in their own area.

The **sheriff** was the king's agent in each county. He would be a powerful lord who would do the king's work without pay, knowing that it gave him great status. He also knew that some of the fines that were paid would come his way. The property of all convicted murderers, including people who had committed suicide, went to the crown as well and the sheriff would take a share. He worked closely with the coroners (see page 15) and with the chief constables (see below). If local groups did not track down criminals, particularly gangs of robbers, the sheriff would call an armed **posse** and search the county for them.

Two **chief constables of the hundred** were appointed each year to supervise law and order in their area. They were usually quite wealthy farmers. They gained local status from taking on this role. Their main duty was to ensure that every free man between the ages of fifteen and sixty was equipped and ready to take up arms and serve the king if needed. This might be in the army or in the sheriff's posse.

The **parish constable** was another one-year appointment. One responsible man in each parish had to take on this role alongside his own full-time work. He had to make sure that his parish could supply armed men when needed. From 1363, he also had to ensure that they practised archery each Sunday. He also had to arrest suspicious strangers. Above all he had to make sure that his village always responded properly to any crime (see below).

The **people** were essential in keeping law and order. Adult men were grouped into tens called tithings. If one of them broke a law the others had to bring him to court. Most importantly, whenever a crime took place the victim had to call for a **hue and cry**. This meant that all within earshot had to stop what they were doing and join in a hunt for the criminal. If a village failed to carry out the hue and cry it would face a huge fine.

▼ The seal of Edward I

◄ A knight, from a thirteenth-century manuscript

▼ Two constables, from a fifteenth-century manuscript

▼ Archers from a thirteenth-century manuscript

▼ Peasants, from a thirteenth-century manuscript

▲ The King's Bench, from a fifteenth-century manuscript

The courts

Royal courts heard the most serious criminal cases. This picture shows a trial at the King's Bench court in London.

- At the bottom stand the criminals awaiting trial. (You also saw them on page 14.)
- At the top sits a row of professional, paid judges.
- Below them are the clerks who record the verdicts.
- The accused stands in the middle with his back to us.
- On the left you can just see the jury.

The jurors were always drawn from the criminal's own area. They took an oath before God and promised to use their local knowledge of the case and of the accused person to decide whether he or she was guilty.

Judges from this court also travelled to counties to try cases but these visits were irregular and inefficient. So, in 1293, King Edward I made an important change. He ordered that royal judges from London would visit each county two or three times a year to try cases of serious crime from that area. These courts were called the **county assizes**, from the French word for sitting. They lasted until 1971.

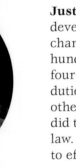

▲ The writer and JP, Geoffrey Chaucer, from a fifteenth-century painting

Justices of the peace (JPs) came into being in 1361 after the role had developed in the previous century. This was an enormously important change. Before then the county sheriff used to run courts in each hundred but these only met twice a year. The king appointed three or four justices of the peace in each county to take over the sheriffs' court duties. They passed really serious cases to the assizes, but judged others in their own courts with a jury of local people. After 1388, they did this four times a year at the **quarter sessions.** JPs enforced royal law. They were unpaid but educated and wealthy. They were essential to effective local law and government for hundreds of years.

Manor courts dealt with most crime in medieval England. Their main task was to run the lord's lands and deal with offences by his villeins, but by 1250 many manors had also taken over the work of the hundred courts. This meant that they judged any petty crimes that affected the whole community. These offences were reported by the tithings, the constable or by individuals. They included thefts, land disputes, fights and debts. The lord or his steward ran the court and juries of wealthier villagers decided each case or passed it to a higher court.

Each manor had its own local laws that had been established over hundreds of years. By 1500, manor courts were losing influence as the king's JPs heard more and more cases. Local laws were fading.

▲ Hawkshead manor court, Cumbria. The court met in the upstairs room of this fifteenth-century building

Law enforcement in the towns

The summary on pages 20 to 21 concentrates on the countryside where most people lived. The same system applied to towns as well but with one or two additions.

Watchmen

King Edward I's Statute of Winchester of 1285 ordered towns to appoint watchmen to patrol the gates and walls at night. Medieval towns could be pitch black at night. Watchmen carried lamps like the one shown here. They had to arrest suspicious strangers and take them to the constable in the morning. They called the hue and cry if they discovered a crime. It was an unpopular job.

Borough courts

This was the name given to the courts run by towns. These had a very similar role to the hundred courts as anyone who lived in a medieval town for over a year was a freeman.

Church courts

All laws and court proceedings in medieval England were based on Christian principles but there were some offences that the Church liked to deal with directly. People who were accused of these offences were tried in courts run by the Church. Many cases concerned offences by priests such as Robert Segefeld. He was tried at Durham in 1455 for having sex with Joan Bell, a married woman. Priests were not supposed to marry, let alone have sex with other men's wives. They obviously found this rule difficult to obey as this type of offence appears often in the records of church courts.

The church court did not just try clergy. Anyone might be put on trial for sex outside marriage, homosexuality, failing to attend church, persistent swearing, gambling or for not knowing the Lord's Prayer. Church courts dealt with the very rare cases of divorce and would certainly want to try anyone accused of holding or spreading false Christian beliefs or of dabbling in witchcraft. There were no juries in these courts. Priests heard the evidence and passed judgment.

Medieval juries

In our day, jury members must not know the accused and must listen to two lawyers who present evidence to try to show whether the accused is guilty or not. The jury considers the evidence and the lawyers' arguments to reach a verdict.

Medieval juries would have found our ways very strange. They were always selected from the same parish or hundred as the person who was accused unless he or she was a visiting stranger. They used their knowledge of the person's character, background and past offences to reach their verdict. They had to know as much as possible about the case before it came to court. Some of their ideas may have been based on rumour or guesswork. The court spent little or no time establishing facts and weighing up arguments. Jurors swore an oath before God that they would not lie. If the jury said someone was guilty or not guilty, the judge accepted their view. The jury knew best and the verdict stood. Few medieval court cases took more than twenty minutes!

▲ A fifteenth-century watchman from an Italian town

Reflect

Now that you know about all the different types of medieval court, look back at some of the cases on pages 15 to 19 and try to decide which type of court would have heard each case.

Record

Make some more crime cards. These could be about:

- why there was no professional police force in the Middle Age
- why every man had to keep deadly weapons
- why villagers might have to stop work and join a hue and cry
- why a crime might be tried in one or more of five different courts
- why juries were expected to know the accused person.

Verdicts

On page 14 you looked at a pie chart showing different types of crime that went to trial in eight English counties between 1300 and 1348. This graph shows what happened in those cases. They were all heard at the county assize by a royal judge, working with local juries.

You will see that for each crime at least half of the accused people were found not guilty – except for treason cases. Juries did not want to upset the king.

Medieval juries were generally very lenient and often let the accused go free in these serious cases, especially if they were women. They were less lenient over petty crimes in manor courts. The reason why juries were reluctant to find people guilty of serious offences may well become clearer in the next section where we learn about the punishments that were used.

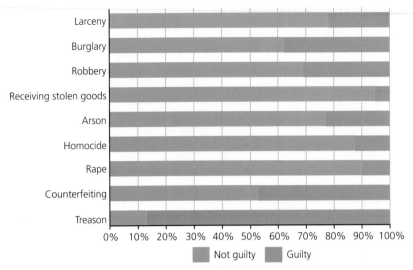

▲ Graph showing the conviction rate of court cases for serious crimes in eight English counties, 1300–48

Record

Make a copy of this table. It follows up ten of the cases on pages 15 to 19. All the people accused of these crimes were found guilty.

On your copy add some more details about each case in the 'Crime' column.

On your copy fill in which type of court you think would have heard each crime.

Page	Year	Crime	Type of court	Punishment
15	1271	Burglary/homicide		
16	1311	Homicide – by a priest		
16	1316	Petty larceny (value 12d) and receiving		
17	1359	Scolding		
18	1402	Robbery		Leave this column empty for now
18	1411	Gambling		
18	1413	Heresy		
19	1420	Treason (murdered her husband – a JP!)		
19	1476	Fraud – selling rancid butter		
19	1477	Public nuisance – left dung heap in road		

Punishments

The four main types punishment between 1250 and 1500 were:

Fines

- All fines from manor courts went to the lord. It was a very effective way of making more money from their land.
- Mayors and town leaders took the fines imposed by borough courts for offences by traders, thieves or even gamblers.
- Church courts imposed fines for sins such as gambling. The Church kept the money.
- Kings received the fines paid at the hundred court and, later, at the quarter sessions. They also received fines from villages that failed to raise a hue and cry. Nobles who disobeyed the king often received a pardon but had to pay a very large fine.

▲ A silver groat from c.1300. This was worth 4d, which would have been a week's wages for many peasants

Public humiliation

- Manor courts sometimes forced women who were scolds to sit in public on a cucking stool, a sort of wooden toilet.
- Borough courts often made traders sit in stocks or stand at a pillory for cheating customers by selling faulty goods. In 1331, people in Lincoln complained that their mayor was fining too many traders and should be using the pillory instead.
- The church court shamed the Durham priest who slept with a man's wife (see page 22). They made him publicly confess his sin out loud at the cathedral's main altar.

Imprisonment

- Prisons were not used as a punishment for serious crimes but a prisoner awaiting trial might spend months in gaol.
- Imprisonment was used to punish debtors, forgers, offenders who could not pay their fines and people who had falsely accused someone at trial.
- Gaols were rough, unhealthy places. Prisoners had to supply all their own bedding, food and drink or buy these from their gaoler. He was unpaid but earned his living from the prisoners. Poor prisoners often sat begging outside the gaol, securely fastened. This was their only way of being able to pay their gaoler.
- Richer prisoners might be kept in quite comfortable rooms in castles as they could afford this.

▼ Criminals on an English street, from a twelfth-century manuscript

Reflect

Use the information about imprisonment on this page to suggest what might be happening in this picture.

Death

All these executions were carried out in public as a warning to all and to show that justice had been done.

- **Hanging** until the criminal was slowly strangled. The neck was rarely broken. This was the punishment for crimes such as
  - murder (deliberate homicide)
  - rape (before 1275 the criminal would not be hanged, just castrated)
  - theft of goods worth more than 12d (from 1275)
  - burglary (even if nothing was stolen)
  - robbery (even if nothing was stolen).

  Over 80 per cent of hangings were for non-violent crimes.

- **Hanging, drawing and quartering.** The criminal was hanged but taken down while still alive to be cut into pieces. This was the punishment for
  - high treason (plotting to kill the king)
  - counterfeiting gold or silver coins.

- **Being burned alive** on a bonfire (bone-fire). This was the punishment for
  - petty treason, such as a wife killing her husband or a servant killing a master
  - heresy, such as the beliefs of the Lollards. (The Church tried to avoid executing people, so the king ordered the Church to send all convicted Lollards to the sheriff who had them burned.)

- **Local variations on hanging** had disappeared by about 1350 but they show how punishments, like laws, often had a local character in the early Middle Ages. Examples include
  - being thrown from the cliffs at Dover
  - being buried alive at Sandwich
  - being tied to a rock at sea in the Scilly Isles. The criminal was left at low tide and given bread and water. As the tide came in he drowned.

In cases of serious crime, all the property of anyone found guilty, whether executed or not, was passed to the king. The innocent victims or their families never regained their valuables.

Reflect

Rulers and governments in all ages consider four main issues when thinking how to punish criminals. They are listed below.

Which of these do you think medieval people considered when they came up with the punishments shown on these pages?

- **Retribution**: making criminals suffer so that they know that their behaviour was wrong.
- **Removal**: allowing society to get on with life free from crime.
- **Rehabilitation**: improving criminals' lives so they avoid crime.
- **Deterrence**: using fear of the consequences to stop people from committing crimes.

▶ A hanging from a Bible story in a fourteenth-century manuscript

Ten ways to cheat death

Naturally, people did all they could to avoid these dreadful punishments. Here are some methods they often used.

To avoid a trial:

1. Run
Criminals who knew they were guilty and who escaped the hue and cry could try to join an outlaw gang in a forest.

2. Seek sanctuary
Churches and cathedrals offered sanctuary to criminals on the run. If they could stay there for forty days and forty nights they would be allowed to confess their crime to a coroner and then 'abjure the realm'. This means they had to leave England forever. While in the church a criminal had to wear a special robe and then travel along an agreed route to a port, carrying a white cross. From there he sailed to a foreign land.

3. Have powerful friends
Most cases were heard first at the manor courts. If the jurors were sympathetic to the accused person they might dismiss the charge or decide that any property stolen was worth less than 12d.

The most powerful of friends was the local lord. They could use retainers to pressurise juries into dropping a charge or simply make sure that the juries were made up of the lord's own supporters.

4. Refuse to plead
Some brave prisoners refused to plead either guilty or not guilty at their trial. They were sent back to gaol and lived on rotten bread and dirty water until they changed their mind. This might lead to a long, slow and unpleasant death anyway, but it saved the family of the accused from having to hand any property to the king.

▲ A twelfth-century door knocker from Durham Cathedral. Any criminal who held the ring on this knocker was given sanctuary

To avoid being condemned to death:

5. Hope for a friendly jury
Jurors at assize courts often found ways of helping the accused. After all, they usually knew the person on trial.

- Even if they believed the accused had stolen or received some valuable property, jurors might give a verdict of not guilty. This was particularly likely for women or if they thought the crime was committed out of desperation. Any stranger accused of serious theft in a village was far more likely to be hanged than a local person.
- In cases of murder, juries might choose to say that the killing was done in self-defence or by accident. If so, the offender was guilty of 'excusable homicide' and would receive a royal pardon. But the king still took all the criminal's property.

In all these cases, the jurors took their oath seriously but they probably trusted God to know that they were trying to be fair.

Reflect

1. Why might juries have been more lenient towards women?
2. Why might the king still take the property of someone he had pardoned for committing 'excusable homicide'?

To avoid being executed even when found guilty:

6. Buy a pardon from the king
This was only possible for the wealthiest people but it happened surprisingly often as kings were always eager for extra money.

7. Join the king's army
In times of war, kings often pardoned outlaws and other criminals if they would agree to serve in his army abroad.

8. Be pregnant
Pregnant women were never executed before having their child. Their sentence was often changed to a fine.

9. Claim benefit of clergy
Royal courts such as the assizes could try priests but they could not punish them. Only the Church could do that and the Church did not execute people. This was known as the 'benefit of clergy'.

As anyone might claim to be a priest to escape death, a law was passed in 1351. It said that anyone who wanted to prove that he was a priest had to read a particular verse from the Bible, begging God for mercy. Some criminals learned the verse by heart so that they could recite it from memory, even if they were illiterate. Educated men could also escape death this way, even if they were not priests. No women gained benefit of clergy as women could not be priests.

After escaping execution, the priest might still be shamed in public or have to abjure the realm and he would lose his property to the king.

10. Become a king's approver
We are back where we started. As you may remember, Walter de Blowberme became an approver and named ten other men who were found guilty of serious crimes. In return, he was allowed to abjure the realm. But a year later he made the mistake of coming back to England and committing another crime. This time there was no escape. He was hanged as a robber in 1250.

Record

Make your final crime cards based on what you have learned about medieval punishments on pages 24 to 25. There are plenty of puzzling punishments and strange ways of avoiding death to choose from.

Review

1. Find the table that you copied from page 23. Use what you have learned about medieval punishments to complete the right-hand column. Check your answers with a friend.
2. Gather all your crime cards and use them to revise and improve your understanding of medieval crime and punishment. You could:
   a. Place the cards 'Puzzle' side up on a table and test how many of the explanations you can remember.
   b. Place the cards 'Explanation' side up and test how many of the puzzles you can recall based on the explanation.
   c. Make a 'chain' that matches a crime with a court and then a punishment.
   d. Group the cards by theme under headings such as 'Property', 'Violence', 'Government' or 'Serious/petty'.
   e. Use the cards to plan a structured essay explaining why medieval crime and punishment may look puzzling but makes more sense when you understand what lies behind it.

An outlaw gang

▲ The tomb of Eustace Folville, at Ashby Folville, Leicestershire

This worn and crumbled fourteenth-century tomb is the resting place of Sir Eustace Folville. With a tomb like this and a name like that, you might well imagine that Eustace was the sort of knight who played an important part in upholding the king's peace in his local area. Perhaps he might have been a lord of the manor or even a sheriff. In fact he was little more than a gangster.

The road to crime

One reason why Eustace took up a life of crime was that he was did not inherit land from his father. Sir John Folville was a wealthy landowner in Leicestershire but when he died, according to the custom of the time, he left all his lands to his oldest son, also called John. This son took over as the lord of the manor and, as far as we know, lived honestly and responsibly all his life.

Eustace did not. Younger sons of landowners usually became soldiers or found employment in the Church. Some even became traders. None of these appealed to Eustace or to his five younger brothers. They teamed up and became a gang of ruthless robbers.

First victim

The first known victim of the Folville Gang was Roger Bellers, an important royal judge who had a reputation for corruption. In 1326, the Folvilles and over forty others ambushed Bellers on the road. Although none of the Folvilles delivered the stab that killed him, they were clearly responsible. A hue and cry went out for their capture but they were not caught. Instead they seem to have escaped to France.

The gang returned in 1327 after the new king, Edward III, issued a pardon. Kings often did this when they took the throne. If it was supposed to gain the loyalty and obedience of the pardoned men it did not work. They set about a whole series of robberies and went into hiding as outlaws.

Amazingly, the brothers received another pardon when they agreed to fight on the king's side against a rebellious earl. During that campaign they took time off to raid the town of Leicester, looting goods worth about £90,000 in today's values.

Over the next three years Eustace alone was accused of three robberies, four murders and a rape. The gang also did some criminal work for the monks of an abbey in Lincolnshire, burning down the watermill of a landowner against whom the monks had a grudge.

Kidnap and ransom

Eustace Folville's most notorious crime came in 1332 when he and the gang kidnapped Sir Richard Willoughby, another of the king's judges. They moved him from place to place as they waited to see if the king would pay the ransom they had demanded. He did. He paid a sum worth about £400,000 today. The Folvilles then let Sir Richard go free but only after Eustace had robbed him of all his personal goods and made him swear an oath of future loyalty to the Folvilles.

The brothers then spent much of the 1330s fighting for the king – after yet another pardon – in Scotland and in France, but they continued to commit all sorts of crimes when they chose to.

Death of an outlaw priest

The law did catch up with one of the brothers. In 1340, Richard Folville became the priest in charge of the church in the Folville manor. Maybe he was after the money that came from the church lands. The king sent a local nobleman to capture Richard who sheltered inside the church and fired arrows at the lord and his men below him in the churchyard. He killed one and seriously injured many more. Eventually the lord broke through the thick church doors and dragged Richard across the churchyard away from the sacred ground, and beheaded him in the street.

Although killing an outlaw was allowed, Richard was a priest. The lord who had killed him was forced to walk around the most important churches in the area to be whipped outside each one. This was his reward for capturing a robber.

▼ A fourteenth-century arrow head

Eustace's last years

Meanwhile Eustace Folville carried on fighting in wars and committing various crimes until he died in 1345 or 1346. He was never brought to court for any of his crimes and was laid to rest beneath a fine monument in his local church.

2

Crime and punishment, 1500–1750

More of the same?

In 1546, Anne Askew, the woman in the portrait below, was executed in a way which seems horrific to us today. She was burnt to death. Anne Askew's crime was heresy – holding religious beliefs which were not allowed by the state. Anne was a follower of Protestantism, the new faith which had spread from Germany to England in the early sixteenth century. King Henry VIII did not approve of Protestantism. He had taken control of the English Church, but the king remained a Catholic. In Henry's England, anyone who preached Protestantism was a heretic and faced death by burning.

Anne Askew was born in 1521 into a wealthy Lincolnshire family. At the age of 15, her father forced her to marry Thomas Kyne, a large landowner in the county. The couple had two children, but their marriage was a disaster mainly because Thomas was a Catholic and did not accept Anne's Protestantism. Anne left her husband and travelled to London where she mixed with other Protestants. In May 1546, Henry VIII ordered 23 people suspected of heresy to be arrested. The group included Anne Askew.

Anne was taken to the Tower of London where she was interrogated and tortured to give the names of other Protestants and to convert back to Catholicism. She was placed on the rack, the most terrifying form of torture in Tudor England. Her wrists and ankles were tied, and the wheel of the rack was slowly turned.

◀ A portrait of Anne Askew, c.1560

Her body was stretched taut a few inches above the base of the rack. Anne's pain is hard to imagine. As the wheel was turned even further Anne's shoulders and hips were pulled out of their sockets and her knees and elbows were dislocated. She gave no names and refused to give up her faith.

On 16 July 1546, Anne Askew was carried to her place of execution at Smithfield in a chair because she could no longer walk. Every movement caused her severe pain. She was placed on a small seat attached to a stake and was securely chained. Three other Protestants were chained next to her. A bishop climbed the steps of a pulpit and preached to them. He gave the prisoners a last chance to convert back to Catholicism. All refused. Watched by a large crowd of people, the executioners piled brushwood around Anne and the other Protestants. They then set the wood alight. It was later reported that Anne was silent at first, only screaming in agony when the flames reached her chest.

Historians do not know exactly when burning at the stake was first used as a punishment in Britain, but the first recorded case was in 1222. Burning was used in the fifteenth century to punish Lollards. In the sixteenth century, after Henry VIII strengthened the heresy laws, the number of burnings increased, particularly during the reign of Mary I (1553–1558).

Burning was used for both male and female heretics. It was also the punishment for women found guilty of treason. The male punishment of hanging, drawing and quartering was thought to be unacceptable for women because it involved nudity. Very few women were burnt at the stake for committing treason, but many were burnt for 'coining' (defacing or forging coins) as this was a treasonable offence. A large number of women were also burnt for petty treason – the murder of a husband. According to the Treason Act of 1351, the murder of a husband by his wife involved betrayal and was therefore a form of treason. Women convicted of petty treason were usually strangled before being burnt. Heretics like Anne Askew were not so lucky – they faced the full horror of being burnt alive.

◄ A sixteenth-century woodcut showing the burning of Anne Askew

The Enquiry

Burning at the stake was a punishment which began in the Middle Ages but which became much more widespread in the sixteenth century. It is a good example of the way in which crime and punishment developed in the period historians call 'early modern', between 1500 and 1750. In the early modern period, there were some significant continuities in crime and punishment, but also some new developments. Your challenge in this enquiry is to make a judgment about exactly how much crime and punishment had changed by 1750. You will focus on changes and continuities in:

1. the nature and extent of crime
2. the way in which the law was enforced
3. the types of punishments which criminals faced.

As you work though the enquiry it would be helpful to summarise the changes and continuities in a chart like the one below.

Early modern crime and punishment		
	Continuities	Changes
Nature and extent of crime		
Enforcing the law		
Punishments		

Before you consider these issues it will be useful to find out about the bigger changes and continuities in early modern England, and to think about how these might have affected crime and punishment ...

Record

The next four pages summarise different aspects of life in Britain, 1500–1750. Read through them quickly and make a list of at least six specific features that you think may have affected crime and punishment at that time. Collect and explain your ideas in a table like this:

Specific feature of life at this time	How I think this may have affected crime and punishment

1. Daily bread

In the period 1500–1750, most people continued to live and work in the countryside. This was a small-scale world of villages and market towns. Local institutions like the manor and the parish played an important part in people's lives, and the farming year set the pattern of work and leisure in the village.

This painting from the early eighteenth century shows men and women harvesting hay on the manor of Dixton in Gloucestershire. As you can see, farming continued to be done by hand and many people were needed to work in the fields at harvest time. If bad weather ruined the harvest there was a shortage of bread and people went hungry. At times of hunger society was under a lot of pressure.

▶ A painting of the harvesters at Dixton, Gloucestershire, early eighteenth century

2. Growing inequalities

Overall, England became a more prosperous country in the period 1500–1750. However, English society was very unequal. Many gentry and 'middling' families became wealthier, building new houses and filling them with fine furnishings. In contrast, life for poor labouring families was often very tough, particularly in the century after 1550. Between 1550 and 1650 the population of England doubled. This led to increasing food prices, falling wages and unemployment. In the 1590s, harvest failure and famine added to the problems of the labouring poor. Many people had no choice but to leave their village and look for work in another part of the country. From around 1650, the population was no longer rising and pressures on the poor began to ease. However, by the eighteenth century, about a third of the population, despite being in work and good health, could still not support themselves and their families without assistance.

◀ A woodcut from the sixteenth century showing a gentleman giving money to a beggar

◄ William Hogarth's 'Gin Lane', 1751

3. Growing towns

Even though most families in early modern England continued to live in the countryside, more and more people moved to the towns to look for work. By 1750, about a fifth of the population lived in towns. But remember that this was a relatively minor change compared to the age of mass urbanisation which occurred in the period 1750–1900. In the early modern period, towns continued to be quite small. London, however, was very different. In the period 1500–1750, London grew into the largest and busiest city in Europe. In 1550, the population of London was around 120,000. By 1750, over 700,000 people lived in the city. London was a city of great wealth, but also of terrible poverty. In the early eighteenth century, hundreds of thousands of poor men and women turned to gin as an escape from the misery of lack of work and poor living conditions. In 1751, the artist William Hogarth showed the evils of London's 'gin craze' in his engraving 'Gin Lane'.

4. New products and duties

This painting shows Bristol docks and quay in the eighteenth century. By 1750, Bristol had become an important trading port and the town had more than doubled in size since 1600. The period from 1600 to 1750 saw a transformation in trade with Europe and the wider world. In the seventeenth and eighteenth centuries, England established colonies in North America and developed a transatlantic trade in slaves, metal goods, sugar and tobacco. In 1608, the East India Company sent its first ship to India and began to trade in cotton, silk, spices and dyes. From the end of the seventeenth century, the government raised much of its income by collecting very high taxes (duties) on imported luxury goods such as tea, tobacco, wine and brandy. Traders who wanted to import luxury goods often had to pay a duty of 30 per cent and this forced up the price for consumers.

▲ A painting of Bristol Quay in the eighteenth century

5. Travel

People in early modern England moved around. Young people moved to work as servants in houses or on farms. Families moved from place to place in search of land or work. 'Drovers' herded their cattle and sheep over long distances to markets in the towns. 'Carriers' took cloth and other goods to the towns by packhorse and cart. For much of the period 1500–1750, people travelled on horseback or by cart. If they were poor, they walked. From the seventeenth century, more roads were built and stagecoach travel became popular. Stagecoaches were horse-drawn carriages that travelled long distances between major towns. They moved goods or passengers around the country, stopping at coaching inns like the one in the picture. The rich paid more to travel inside the coach while poorer people faced the weather on top of the coach. There were few banks so wealthy people often carried their money and jewellery with them when they travelled by stagecoach.

▲ An eighteenth-century stagecoach

6. Government

In the early modern period, the government increased its power over the people. This began with the Tudor monarchs who ruled England between 1509 and 1603. When Henry VIII became king in 1509, he insisted that people called him 'Your Majesty', a title which English kings had never used before. This famous portrait of Henry by Hans Holbein shows us how the king projected his power through art. During the 1530s and early 1540s, Henry created a much more efficient bureaucracy which ensured that his revenues increased. He also used Parliament to introduce many new laws. Under Henry's children who ruled after him (Edward, 1547–53; Mary, 1553–58; Elizabeth, 1558–1603) the power of the state grew even stronger. People's lives became more closely controlled by the government.

◀ A portrait of Henry VIII in 1540 by Hans Holbein, the younger

7. State religion

In the sixteenth and seventeenth centuries, religion continued to play an important part in people's lives. But, from the 1530s, the Reformation led to bitter divisions in the Church. These are the ruins of Glastonbury Abbey in Somerset, the largest of over 500 monasteries in England at the end of the Middle Ages. Between 1536 and 1540, Henry VIII and his chief minister, Thomas Cromwell, closed Glastonbury and all the other monasteries in England. The dissolution of the monasteries was part of a wider Reformation of the Church in Europe. Protestants objected to the power of the Catholic Church. They argued that priests and bishops had become corrupt and that only by reading the Bible could people find true faith. Some people in England remained Catholics, others became Protestants. However, *all* people were expected to follow the official state religion chosen by the monarch.

▼ The ruins of Glastonbury Abbey, Somerset

8. Puritans

In the later sixteenth century, a group of Protestants emerged who wanted to take the Reformation even further – the Puritans. Puritans wanted to purify the Church of all traces of the old Catholic religion. They believed that many people were living sinful lives and that only by following the teachings of the Bible could people become closer to God. In parts of England where Puritanism was strong, preachers, justices of the peace and constables tried to enforce higher standards of Christian behaviour. The Puritans were concerned about people who did not attend church on Sundays, preferring to work, or spend their time in the alehouse instead. Drinking, dancing, gambling, swearing and sex outside marriage were all seen as sinful by Puritans.

◀ A portrait of the Puritan scholar and writer Richard Baxter, 1670

▲ The execution of Charles I, by an unknown artist, c.1649

9. New rulers

The middle of the seventeenth century was a terrible time in Britain. Between 1642 and 1648 King Charles I and Parliament fought bitter civil wars over how England should be ruled. The Civil War divided the country and caused huge disruption and suffering in many villages and towns. Tens of thousands of people were killed in battles fought across the country. Parliament eventually defeated the king and placed him on trial for making war on his own people. This painting shows the execution of Charles I on 30 January 1649. Following the execution, England was ruled as a republic until the monarchy was eventually restored in 1660. During the 1650s, Puritans, led by Oliver Cromwell, were in control of the country.

10. Power in the localities

This painting from 1670 shows Sir Henry Tichborne handing out bread to the poor people on his manor in Hampshire. Large landowners like Sir Henry Tichborne played an important part in running their county, just as they had done in the Middle Ages. In each county, men from landowning families became MPs and were appointed as justices of the peace, enforcing the law and acting as administrators. After the Restoration in 1660, the monarchy had limited power. The country was ruled by the large landowners who became MPs by gaining the support of the few people who were allowed to vote. The priorities for these wealthy landowners were keeping the country stable and protecting their property.

▲ 'The Tichborne Dole', a painting from 1670

11. The power of print

The printing press, which was introduced into Britain at the end of the fifteenth century, transformed people's lives. For centuries, monks had carefully copied individual manuscripts onto parchment. From the sixteenth century, multiple copies on paper could be made quickly and cheaply. This made the work of national and local government much more effective. It also meant that people had access to a wide range of printed books and pamphlets. In early modern England, more people learned to read and write. They were eager to read news of local and national events. Broadsheets (early newspapers) first emerged druing the Civil War. By 1750, there were four daily newspapers in London, and over thirty newspapers were published in different towns across the country.

◄ 'The London Post', a seventeenth-century newspaper

Crimes and criminals in the early modern period

Historians researching the nature and extent of crime in the period 1500–1750 have made four interesting discoveries:

Record

When you have read about these four discoveries, remember to summarise the changes and continuities in your 'Early modern crime and punishment' chart. Look back at 'The Enquiry' on page 31 for details.

1. **The violence and disorder that was common among late medieval nobles declined.** As you discovered in the first enquiry, murder, robbery, rape and assault were often part of the feuds between the supporters of rival nobleman in the later Middle Ages. By 1550, the nobility and gentry were less likely to be involved in organised crime of this type. Landowners increased their income by improving their estates, or by investing in trade, rather than by robbing their neighbours. From the late sixteenth century, the nobility and gentry began to settle their disputes by duelling (fighting individually with swords or guns) rather than by feuding.

2. **The types of crime committed by ordinary people in the early modern period were similar to those of the Middle Ages.** Historians have to be careful when trying to measure crime because some types of crime may not be reported, but it seems that there was a low level of serious crime in the early modern period. As in the Middle Ages, the most common serious crimes were property offences rather than crimes against the person. Another continuity was that petty crimes continued to be far more common than serious crime. The theft of low value items, often committed by poor people when the price of bread was high, was the most common crime in the early modern period, just as it had been in the Middle Ages.

3. **There was a dramatic rise in crime from the middle of the sixteenth century and then a huge fall in the crime rate from the middle of the seventeenth century.** One historian used court records from the county of Cheshire to calculate crime figures for theft and murder from 1580 to 1709. You can see from these graphs that there was a clear pattern of rise and fall in both types of crime during the early modern period. Historians have linked the rise in crime from the late sixteenth century to the huge increase in population, rising prices and falling wages. In the period 1650–1750, the country was under less pressure and the crime rate went down.

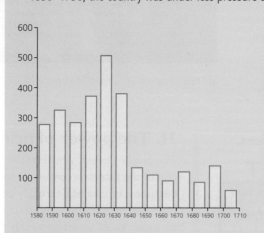

▲ A graph showing changes in the rate of theft and other property offences in Cheshire, 1580–1710

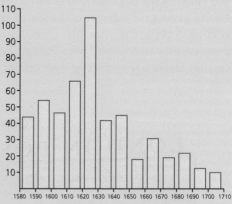

▲ A graph showing changes in the murder rate in Cheshire, 1580–1710

4. **Certain types of crime were seen as big problems in the early modern period.** In the sixteenth and seventeenth centuries, the authorities were particularly concerned about vagrancy, moral crimes and witchcraft. By the eighteenth century, Britain's rulers were more worried about crimes such as smuggling and highway robbery. We need to find out why these particular crimes caused so much concern in the early modern period …

Record

Over the next five pages you will find out the types of crime which caused concern in the early modern period. For each one:

1. Draw a cartoon to help you remember the type of crime.
2. Around each cartoon list the reasons why people were concerned about this type of crime.

Vagrancy

In the late sixteenth century, life became very difficult for poor labourers and their families. The underlying reason for this was a growth in population. The number of people in England rose from around 2.4 million in 1520 to 4.1 million in 1600. This increase in population caused a rapid rise in prices. In particular, the wages of poor labourers failed to keep up with the rising price of their staple food – bread. The pressure on the poor was particularly bad in years when the harvests failed because of bad weather, or when a downturn in demand for English woollen cloth put many people out of work. At these times, many people had no choice but to leave their villages and become vagrants. In the Middle Ages, many people did not have the freedom to leave their manor, but by the 1600s these restrictions could no longer be enforced. Large numbers of vagrants began to wander between villages and towns, searching for work, begging and sometimes stealing to survive.

Growing concerns

People became very concerned about the problem of vagrancy in Elizabethan England. Printed pamphlets and books horrified people with sensational accounts of vagrants wandering in large gangs and committing thefts, assaults and murders. In 1567, Thomas Harman wrote a book warning people about the dangerous 'rogues' and 'vagabonds' roaming the country. On this page from Harman's book you can see two of the 23 different types of vagabond he described and illustrated. On the left is an 'upright man', a vagabond who pretended to be a respectable man. On the right is a 'counterfeit crank' who, according to Harman, pretended to be ill by eating soap and foaming at the mouth.

▲ A page from Thomas Harman's book warning about vagabonds, 1568

The printing press, and an increase in literacy, meant that many people were able to read pamphlets and books like Harman's in the early modern period. These new forms of communication influenced people's attitudes and helped to make vagrants the criminal stereotype of the sixteenth century. In reality, vagrants rarely travelled in large gangs, and few of them were criminals. Most vagrants who appeared before the courts were far less threatening than the popular books and pamphlets suggested. They nearly all travelled alone or in twos and threes. Most were desperate people in search of any work they could find. It was not vagrants but poor people in general who were often driven to theft because of the misery of their lives.

Record

Draw your first cartoon and list the reasons why people were so concerned about vagrants in the sixteenth and seventeenth centuries.

Reflect

1. Which of the offences below would still be considered a crime today?
2. Why do you think the Puritan leaders of Dorchester were so concerned about these 'crimes'?

Moral crime

Growing Puritan influence in the late sixteenth century led to an increased concern about people's sinful behaviour. In some villages and towns, Puritan preachers and respectable people tried to create well-ordered and 'godly' communities by punishing moral crimes such as drinking, swearing and sexual immorality. In the early seventeenth century, the small town of Dorchester became a Puritan stronghold. The historian David Underdown, who wrote a book about Puritan Dorchester, discovered many interesting cases of people who appeared before Dorchester's courts for their sinful behavior. Some of these cases are shown below.

In March 1637, several people were dancing, singing and drinking through the night at John Brine's house.

A neighbour heard John Facey swear at his son saying 'A pox take thee'.

The blacksmith Methuselah Notting was a drunkard. When his wife pleaded with him to stop drinking he beat her up, insisting on his right to do as he pleased.

Jasper Brewer's alehouse was closed in 1631 when one of his servants became pregnant by a customer.

Susan Lee had an affair with Francis Churchill, a miller, while her husband was away at Woodbury Hill Fair. A neighbour heard them making love in the barn.

Henry Hobbes and Hugh Haggard were fined for talking in the street when they should have been attending the church service.

Robert Sampson, a shoemaker, and John Chimney, a glover, worked together between 1627 and 1629 to steal chickens, grain, clothing and fuel from people in Dorchester and surrounding villages. Sampson even stole clothes from his mother-in-law.

Mary Collinford was ducked in the river because she called Elizabeth Lugge 'gig, runagate, speakearse and baggage'.

In 1617, some schoolboys were caught drinking at an alehouse run by Nicholas Hellier.

At the weaver Thomas Chapman's house, an apprentice and young female servant made love in the cellar.

In church one Sunday, Giles Morey stuffed dirt down the back of William Pouncey's shirt.

One Sunday afternoon, Andrew Fooke and Robert Gillet went to Bockington with their girlfriends to eat cream.

A view of Dorchester in the late nineteenth century

Witchcraft

◀ The execution of witches in Newcastle-upon-Tyne, from Ralph Gardner, *England's Grievance Discovered in Relation to the Coal Trade* (London, 1655)

Reflect

Look carefully at the details in the picture. What can this source tell us about attitudes towards witchcraft in the seventeenth century?

This picture from a 1655 pamphlet shows the execution of a group of women in Newcastle-upon-Tyne. The women were hanged for a crime which does not exist in Britain today – witchcraft.

In medieval England, witches were sometimes put on trial in the church courts, but it seems that there were few cases overall and witches were never executed. In the sixteenth and early seventeenth centuries, the government introduced harsh new laws against witchcraft and the number of witchcraft accusations rose dramatically. It is difficult to give an exact figure for the number of witches who were executed under the new laws because records do not survive everywhere, but it is likely that hundreds of women were executed for witchcraft in early modern England.

In south-east England, where many documents of witchcraft trials survive, changes in the number of trials over time give us some clues about what lay behind the concern about witchcraft. In the 1580s and 1590s, when people were suffering much hardship because of famine and plague, the number of witchcraft trials increased dramatically. During the English Civil War (1642–49), there was another big increase, particularly in those areas controlled by the Puritans. By the early 1700s, when educated people were developing scientific ideas about the world which undermined beliefs in magic, witchcraft trials declined.

Detailed research on witchcraft trials gives us more clues about why there was such concern about witchcraft in the period 1500–1650. At that time, there was a widespread belief in magic and the Devil. People believed that the Devil gave witches evil powers through 'familiars' – spirits in the form of small animals which fed on the witch's blood. Witchcraft cases often began with a quarrel between a villager and a poor, elderly woman who made a nuisance of herself. The woman was then accused of causing harm, such as the death of an animal or the sickness of a child. Often, the people making accusations of witchcraft were the richer and more respectable members of the community.

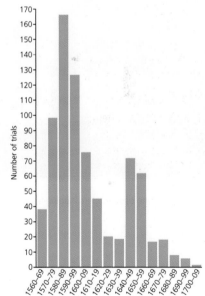

▲ Graph showing the number of witchcraft trials in south-east England, 1560–1709

Record

Draw and annotate cartoons to summarise moral crime and witchcraft. Do not make your moral crime cartoon too rude or the Puritans will be offended.

Organised crime

At about two o'clock on the morning of 3 November 1680, Robert Robinson, a partially-sighted elderly gentleman who lived in a remote house in Westmorland, got the shock of his life. Six men, armed with swords, their faces covered in masks, broke into his house. The robbers forced open a chest in Robert's chamber and stole £43, three silver spoons, a pair of shoes and other goods. Over the next three and a half years this criminal gang, led by two brothers, was involved in burglary from houses and shops, counterfeiting coins, stealing horses and cows, and assault.

Criminal gangs like this continued to operate in the early modern period just as they had in the Middle Ages. However, two new types of organised crime caused particular concern: smuggling and highway robbery.

▲ An engraving of smugglers landing barrels

Smuggling

In the seventeenth and eighteenth centuries, smuggling became a big problem in many coastal areas. At that time, the government depended on import taxes (duties), rather than on income tax, for much of its revenue. Import duties protected British agriculture and industry from competition by forcing up the price of goods from abroad. Smugglers could make a lot of money by secretly bringing goods into the country without paying import duties. In the seventeenth century, tobacco from Virginia was the main item which they smuggled. From the 1720s, when the government increased the duties on brandy, tea and silk to 30 per cent, it was these goods which attracted smugglers. On dark nights, quiet coves and beaches along Britain's south coast were often used by smuggling gangs.

A typical smuggling operation involved a large gang of forty or fifty people. A 'venturer' provided the money to buy the goods in France or Holland. A ship's captain and crew brought them across the English Channel. 'Landers' brought the goods ashore in small boats. Other smugglers carried the contraband to a cave or to someone's barn where it could be hidden. Local people acted as lookouts. At a safe time, carters took the goods to the nearest large town and sold the them to trusted buyers. Respectable people often became involved in smuggling because they disliked the government's high import duties and saw it an easy way to make money. For poor labourers, one night's smuggling could provide them with the same amount of money as they would earn for a week's honest work.

Smuggling gangs often enjoyed support from people in the local area. Many people were reluctant to report smugglers because they did not see smuggling as a crime. Others were afraid of the consequences if they reported smugglers to customs officers. Smuggling gangs often contained criminals who would use violence in order to avoid capture. In 1746, when a customs officer helped to seize 2 tons of tea and 39 barrels of rum smuggled by the notorious Hawkhurst gang, some of the smugglers murdered him.

Highway robbery

Medieval travellers were sometimes robbed by outlaws, but highway robbery became much more common in the early modern period. It was during the reign of Queen Elizabeth I (1558–1603) that the government first became concerned about gangs of robbers on horseback attacking people as they travelled along the roads, particularly around London. During the seventeenth and eighteenth centuries, more roads were built, coach travel became common and the number of travellers increased. Because there were few banks, people often carried money and jewellery with them when they travelled by stagecoach. As people travelled along unlit roads, through forests and remote areas, they were an easy target for highway robbers.

In later periods of history, highwaymen were often portrayed in books, plays and pictures as well-dressed 'gentleman' villains who stole from the rich to help the poor, and who refused to rob women. The reality was very different. Highwaymen were often thugs who committed brutal crimes. One highwayman was hanged after he robbed and then raped a farmer's wife. Another young highwayman called Raby cut off the finger of a woman who refused to give up her ring. In 1722, when a woman said that she knew the identity of three men she saw robbing a stagecoach, the highwaymen cut out her tongue. No wonder people were so concerned about highway robbery in the eighteenth century.

◄ A romantic painting of a highwayman. William Powell Frith's 'Claude Duval', 1860

Record

Draw and annotate cartoons to summarise smuggling and highway robbery. Remember to complete the first part of your 'Early modern crime and punishment' chart to show changes and continuities in the nature and extent of crime.

Reflect

How do the pictures give a 'romantic' image of smuggling and highway robbery?

Enforcing the law

Many features of the medieval system of law enforcement continued into the early modern period. There was still no professional police force and local communities therefore continued to police themselves. It was still individual victims of crime who made the decision to prosecute someone. As in the Middle Ages, if the constable raised the hue and cry, people were expected to turn out and search for a criminal. In the period 1500–1750, law enforcement continued to be administered by unpaid and amateur officials: JPs, constables and churchwardens. As you can see on the opposite page, the structure of the courts was also similar to that of the Middle Ages.

In law enforcement, it is the continuities between the medieval and early modern periods which are most striking, but some significant changes *did* occur. The office of sheriff became much less important as the government extended the role of JPs. As towns grew in size, some began to employ watchmen to patrol the streets and arrest drunks, vagabonds and other criminals. Perhaps the most important change came in the period after 1660 when local manor courts and church courts declined. From the late seventeenth century more criminals were dealt with by JPs at the petty sessions.

Record

Read about the main types of early modern court on the page opposite and then decide which court may have dealt with each of the following early modern offenders. The offences were committed between 1580 and 1700. In the panel below, you can record your suggestions in a list like this one:

1. Owning a pigsty too close to neighbours – manorial court

Cornelius Duckett's neighbours complained that his smelly pigsty was too close to their houses.

One Sunday, instead of attending church, John Ayley invited a fiddler to play at his house.

Elizabeth Codwill, a mentally ill woman, murdered her illegitimate child.

Catherine Jackson was expecting a baby, but was not yet married to her boyfriend, Richard Chapman.

Jacob Halsey was accused of highway robbery.

Mary Panell was accused of bewitching a man to death at his home in Yorkshire.

In the harsh winter of 1623–24, Robert Whitehead, a poor husbandman, stole a sheep to feed his seven children.

Osias Hohnson assaulted one of the parish constables in his village.

John Clark was accused of adultery with Robert Allen's wife.

Robert Wright was in trouble for taking vagrants into his house.

◄ William Lambarde, a Justice of the Peace in Kent, c.1600

Early modern courts

The assizes

These were the country's main courts for dealing with serious offences. By 1550, the country was divided into six 'circuits' and two judges were sent out to hold assizes at different towns in each circuit twice a year. From the late sixteenth century, most of the more serious crimes – murder, manslaughter, grand larceny (the theft of goods worth more than one shilling), burglary, highway robbery, arson, rape and witchcraft – were tried at the assizes. These crimes were 'capital offences' which could result in a death sentence.

The quarter sessions

Four times a year, all the JPs in a county met to try less serious criminal offences. Most of the criminals who appeared before the JPs were accused of petty theft (stealing goods worth less than a shilling). During the reign of Queen Elizabeth I (1558–1603), JPs were given more powers such as fixing wages, organising road-mending, licensing alehouses, regulating local games such as football and arresting vagrants.

Petty sessions

In the seventeenth century it became clear that the volume of work undertaken by JPs could not be carried out if they met only four times a year. In many parts of England, small groups of JPs met more regularly in their local areas. Much of the work of JPs at the petty sessions was administrative, but they also dealt with some types of petty crime such as drunkenness or minor forms of violence.

Manorial courts

Manorial courts continued to play an important role in controlling the behaviour of people on different manors. Tenants who let their animals stray, who stole wood from the common or who got into a fight with a neighbour could all be forced to appear before the manorial court jurors. During the seventeenth century, manorial courts became less important as the petty sessions took over their work.

Church courts

The church courts survived the Reformation and became particularly active in the late sixteenth and early seventeenth centuries. They were concerned not only with enforcing church attendance, but also with keeping up standards of Christian behaviour. People who committed sexual offences, who got drunk on a Sunday or who swore at their neighbours could all be brought before the church courts.

Record

Start the second section of your 'Early modern crime and punishment' chart to summarise changes and continuities in law enforcement.

Controlling the community

In order to really understand how the law was enforced in the early modern period we need to find out what was happening in the villages and small towns where 90 per cent of the people lived. Historians who have researched individual communities have made some interesting findings about the work of law enforcers in the period 1500–1750:

1. Because there was no professional police force, individual communities were expected to police themselves. The system depended on local men who were appointed for one or two years as churchwardens, constables and overseers of the poor. These officials were unpaid and untrained. They often came from wealthier families in the village. It was not only the poor who committed crimes – the local officials were sometimes trouble-makers and criminals themselves.

2. The enforcement of the law in local communities was flexible because the law enforcers often knew the people they were dealing with. Most people who appeared before the courts did so rarely – often only once. Persistent offenders were a bigger challenge, but law enforcers dealt flexibly with people who were often in trouble. They were often able to defuse situations before they got out of hand.

3. Law enforcers relied on local people to help them in their work. Because there was no police force, prosecutions often began with accusations from individual people who were victims of crime, or by people who were offended by a neighbour's behaviour. In the early modern period, it became more common for wealthier villagers to make accusations against their poorer neighbours.

Reflect

1. What aspects of early modern law enforcement made it effective?
2. What aspects made it ineffective?

▶ A list of people who served as Petty Constables and Headboroughs (who were the same as, but slightly less important than the Petty Constables) for Rotherhithe in 1747

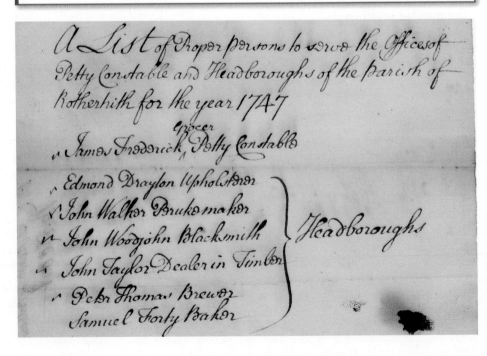

Reflect

Read these three case studies of law enforcement in early modern villages. Analyse each one to find evidence which supports one or more of the findings on page 44.

Case study 1: John Ayley – a trouble-maker and constable

John Ayley was an innkeeper in the village of Kelvedon Easterford in Essex. In the early seventeenth century, the churchwardens often presented Ayley at the church court. They reported him for not attending church in 1613, 1614 and 1622. Nearly every year in the 1620s, Ayley was presented for allowing bad behaviour at his inn or for selling drink on a Sunday. Ayley was also brought before the church court for being drunk and for swearing, and sexual crimes featured in his court appearances. In 1627, villagers reported him for 'immoral living' with his servant Avis Shepheard. The relationship was still causing offence to people in 1631. By 1635, he was accused of chasing another woman – the wife of John Francis. He denied this and was asked by the church court to find eleven witnesses to support his good name. Despite all this trouble, John Ayley was chosen as a constable in 1631.

Case study 2: Grace Payne – accused of theft

Grace Payne was the daughter of William Payne, a poor shoemaker and labourer in the village of Terling in Essex. Members of the Payne family were often in trouble. Grace's father frequently appeared at the church courts for drunkenness. Other members of the family found themselves in trouble for having sex before marriage, for failing to attend church and for not paying the parish rate. In 1600, during a Sunday service in Terling church, Elizabeth Belsted, the wife of a blacksmith, publicly accused Grace Payne of stealing gloves, an apron and a handkerchief from her. Elizabeth Belsted was known to the churchwardens as a troublemaker. She had been presented at the church court for lewd dancing on the village green. At other times, she was accused of causing trouble between her neighbours. The churchwardens, Joseph Cavell and John Burchard, had connections with the Payne family. They decided to do nothing about Grace Payne, but to prosecute Elizabeth Belsted for causing a disturbance in church.

Case study 3: Elizabeth Crossley – accused of witchcraft

Henry Cockroft was a member of a wealthy yeoman family living in the village of Heptonstall in Yorkshire. On 31 December 1646, Henry gave evidence to two JPs about the activities of a poor woman called Elizabeth Crossley. He told them that Elizabeth had come to his house begging, but had left displeased with what Henry's wife had given her. That night Henry's son, aged a year and three-quarters, fell sick with strange fits. Three months later he died. Henry suspected witchcraft, but did not at first link his son's death to the incident with Elizabeth Crossley. Instead, he confronted and beat another woman suspected of witchcraft in Heptonstall, Mary Midgley. She confessed to being a witch, but put the blame for Henry's son's death on Elizabeth Crossley. At Elizabeth Crossley's trial, other villagers from Heptonstall reported that members of their family had been bewitched by her. She was found guilty and hanged.

Record

Complete the second part of your 'Early modern crime and punishment' chart to show changes and continuities in law enforcement.

Punishments

In the early modern period, the most common type of punishment for minor offences was one which courts had used in the Middle Ages – a fine. Manorial courts, petty sessions and quarter sessions all fined people for their wrongdoings. People faced fines for a wide range of offences such as playing unlawful games, minor assaults and small thefts.

Shaming and physical punishments

Other punishments were intended to shame the offender or to cause them physical pain. Offenders were punished in public places in order to cause maximum humiliation and to deter others from offending. Some of these shaming and physical punishments had been used in the Middle Ages, but they became more widespread in the sixteenth and early seventeenth centuries as crime increased. Others were new.

Public penance

In 1631, Ursula Green, a woman from Charminster in Dorset, was found guilty of fornication (having sex outside marriage) with Christopher Harbyn. The court punished Ursula by making her perform public penance in the parish church during the service one Sunday morning. Ursula stood at the front of the church, covered only in a white sheet and holding a white rod. She spoke the following words:

> I do before almighty God and you his church and congregation here present, acknowledge and confess that I have most grievously offended his heavenly Majesty in committing the wicked and detestable offence of fornication with Christopher Harbyn, for which offence I am heartily sorry …

Public penance had been used as a punishment in the Middle Ages, but it became more common in the period 1560–1660.

Pillory

The pillory was another punishment from the Middle Ages which became more widespread in the early modern period. It was often used for people who had traded unfairly or had committed sexual offences. Offenders had their head and arms secured in a wooden frame. People often pelted them with rotten food, offal or animal excrement. When stones were thrown, offenders sometime lost an eye or were even killed. Additional punishments such as branding, nose-slitting or the slicing of ears were occasionally carried out while the offender as in the pillory.

Cucking stools and ducking stools

Cucking stools were used to punish disorderly women, scolds and dishonest tradesmen. They had been used in the Middle Ages but became more common in the second half of the sixteenth century. The offender was tied to a sort of wooden toilet and paraded around the village or town. Ducking stools, first recorded in the seventeenth century, were a harsher punishment. The offender was fastened into a wooden chair with an iron band. The chair was fixed to a long wooden beam so that it could be lowered into a river or pond. Repeated duckings sometimes led to people dying of shock or drowning.

▼ A seventeenth-century print of a ducking stool

Stocks

In the Middle Ages and early modern period, many towns and villages had stocks. Stocks were built in public places such as markets in order to add to the humiliation of the offender. Heavy pieces of wood were placed around the offender's ankles and their feet were locked in place. Offenders were often insulted, spat on or kicked. People who were kept in the stocks for several days and nights in the cold and rain sometimes died of exposure.

Whipping and branding

Whipping had been used in the Middle Ages but it became much more widespread in the late sixteenth century as the problem of vagrancy increased. Branding and mutilation were also used against vagabonds. From 1572, the law stated that vagabonds above the age of fourteen should be whipped and burned through the ear with a hot iron – the hole was to be as big as a penny.

Scold's bridle

Women who were accused of scolding (arguing in public or nagging their husbands) could be forced to wear a scold's bridle. A heavy iron frame was locked onto the woman's head. A projecting spike pressed down on her tongue when the bridle was closed. The scold's bridle was first used in Scotland in the sixteenth century and in England in the seventeenth century. It was an unofficial punishment used by some manorial and church courts.

▼ An engraving of a man leading a woman in a scold's bridle, c.1750

Prisons and bridewells

In the period 1500–1750, prisons continued to be a much less common form of punishment than fines, shaming and physical punishments. As in the Middle Ages, gaols were mainly used to hold prisoners who were in debt, or who were awaiting execution or another form of punishment. Castles, town gates and bridges continued to be used as prisons. In the sixteenth century, Tudor governments began to pass laws to regulate prisons. The 1531 Gaol Act, for example, forced JPs to build a prison where one was needed. As a result, some new prisons were built in the early modern period. But, even by 1750, most prisoners were debtors or people awaiting punishment. The use of prison sentences as a common form of punishment would not begin until the middle of the nineteenth century.

One form of punishment in the early modern period was a totally new development – the bridewell. As you know, in the late sixteenth century, the authorities became very concerned about the problem of vagrancy. In the 1550s, the city of London adopted a new approach to dealing with the problem of crime and poverty. Bridewell Palace was an unused royal palace just outside London's city walls. In 1556, it was turned into a prison. You can see from the engraving below that the palace was a huge building arranged around two courtyards. Here, in these palatial surroundings, vagrants were forced to work. Those who refused faced physical punishment. During the late sixteenth century, bridewells (also known as 'houses of correction') began to appear in many towns. In 1609, the Vagabond Act forced JPs in every county to build bridewells.

Record

Start the final part of your 'Early modern crime and punishment' chart to show changes and continuities in punishment.

▼ An eighteenth-century engraving of Bridewell

47

▲ A seventeenth-century engraving of the execution of the Gunpowder Plotters

Reflect

What details of hanging, drawing and quartering can you find in this seventeenth-century print of the execution of the Gunpowder Plotters?

Capital punishment

In early modern England, people found guilty of the most serious crime, treason, were nearly always executed. Noblemen and gentleman had their heads chopped off with an axe but common people who committed treason were sentenced to hanging, drawing and quartering. This was a gruesome medieval punishment which became much more widespread during the political upheavals of the sixteenth and seventeenth centuries. The condemned man was tied to a hurdle which was dragged to the place of execution by a horse. He was then hanged, but was cut down before he died. First, his penis and testicles were cut off. Then his stomach was slit open. The intestines and heart were cut out and burned in front of the victim. Finally, the head was cut off and the body was cut into four quarters. These were parboiled so they did not rot too quickly and were then displayed on the city gates as a warning to others.

Capital offences other than treason were punished by hanging, just as they had been in the Middle Ages. Hangings took place in major towns and were often watched by large crowds. The condemned person was taken in a cart to the gallows where a noose was placed around their neck. Often, several people were hanged at the same time. There was no sudden drop to break the neck in an instant. This would not be introduced until the late eighteenth century. Instead, the condemned person suffered a slow and agonising death as the noose slowly squeezed life out of them. People were seen to struggle for up to three minutes before dangling limp on the end of the rope.

The Bloody Code

The number of offences for which people could be hanged rose dramatically from the late seventeenth century. Between 1688 and 1820, the government created a ferocious legal system which became known as the Bloody Code. In 1688, rich landowners and merchants increased their power to make laws in parliament. With no police force to protect their property, MPs used the threat of capital punishment to frighten people into being law-abiding citizens. They believed that the fear of hanging would act as a strong deterrent. The number of capital offences gradually increased, from about 50 in 1688 to 200 in 1820. Most of these were for crimes against property. In 1723, the Black Act made the poaching of deer, rabbit and fish a capital offence. Even being caught in a forest at night with a blacked-up face could result in hanging.

Given the huge increase in the number of capital crimes under the Bloody Code, it seems odd that the number of hangings decreased from the middle of the seventeenth century. In Elizabethan Essex, for example, 26 per cent of people accused of a capital offence were hanged, whereas in the early eighteenth century the figure was only 10 per cent. All over the country, levels of executions were much higher in the period 1550–1650 than in the first half of the eighteenth century when the Bloody Code was in force. It seems that assize judges and juries were often unwilling to pass a sentence of hanging for minor crimes. Sometimes they reduced the value of goods stolen to below that of a capital crime. Judges often acquitted defendants because there was insufficient evidence. From the middle of the seventeenth century, they frequently sentenced people to transportation to one of England's colonies in North America or the West Indies, rather than to execution by hanging.

▲ A seventeenth-century woodcut of a hanging

Record

Complete the final section of your 'Early modern crime and punishment' chart.

Review

A At the start of this enquiry you listed at least six features of early modern life and how you thought they might have affected crime and punishment. Go back to that chart and review what you wrote in the light of what you have learned since then. Add some more examples and explanations of how features of early modern life mentioned in the overview on pages 32–35 affected crime and punishment.

B The final question in your exam paper is the most challenging because it asks you to make a judgement. Use your notes from the first two enquiries to answer the following question:
'The most striking thing about medieval and early modern punishments is the continuity of so many aspects'. How far do you agree with this statement? Give reasons for your answer.

An execution at Tyburn

The artist William Hogarth produced this engraving of an execution at Tyburn in 1747. It is the last in a series of pictures which tell the story of two apprentices, one hard-working and the other lazy. The lazy apprentice, Tom Idle, is drawn into crime and eventually commits murder. The engraving shows Tom's execution at the gallows at Tyburn, where Marble Arch stands in London today.

Find the following details in Hogarth's engraving:

- Tom being taken to Tyburn in a cart. He is leaning against his own coffin. The clergyman with him is trying to get him to repent.
- A clergyman in a coach. The clergyman is from Newgate Prison where Tom has been kept. He makes money by writing about the prisoners who are executed.
- Pickpockets.

- A ballad-seller. She is selling a ballad about Tom's last dying speech. These were often written before the speech had been made!
- The grandstand of spectators who had paid to get a better view.
- A man in the grandstand releasing a bird carrying news of the execution to the centre of London.
- Drunken men fighting.
- A man holding a dog by its tail. He is taking aim before he throws it at the cart.

Hogarth disapproved of public executions. Identify the different ways he showed his disapproval in this engraving.

▲ 'The Idle Apprentice', an engraving by William Hogarth, 1747

3

All change

Why was there so much change in crime, policing and punishment, 1750–1900?

▶ An official record from 1873

Reflect

This document from 1873 makes sad reading today. Analyse the document carefully. What interesting details does it contain? Why do you think it was made?

An official record from 1873 for John Hearn, No. 5722, dated 14 June 73.

Name. No. _John Hearn 5722_
and Aliases.

Description:
- Age (on discharge) — 12
- Height — 4 ft 6½
- Hair — Lt. Brown
- Eyes — Blue
- Complexion — Fresh
- Where born — Lambeth
- Married or Single — Single
- Trade or occupation — Errand boy
- Distinguishing marks — None

Address at time of apprehension — 151 Regent St. Lambeth Walk

Place and date of conviction — Lambeth 29 May 73.
Offence for which convicted — Simple Larceny — J. 0. a. Stg 11 pieces of leather 2/-
Sentence — 1 Cal. Mth. H.L.
Date to be liberated — 28 June 73
Intended residence after liberation — As above

Previous Convictions:
- Summary
- By Jury

Remarks antecedents &c.

In May 1873, John Hearn, a twelve-year-old boy from Lambeth, in London, was caught stealing eleven small pieces of leather worth two shillings (10p). John worked as an errand boy, so perhaps he stole the leather from a workshop when he was making a delivery. As a punishment, he was sentenced to one month's hard labour in Wandsworth prison. The document is the charge sheet which was written for John Hearn on 14 June 1873. As you can see, it included a photograph of John with his prison number on a piece of string around his neck – 5722. We will never know what was going through John Hearn's mind when this photograph was taken, but he must surely have felt regret at stealing the leather pieces – or at least at having been caught.

Wandsworth prison, where John Hearn was locked up during June 1873, was the main prison for south London. It had opened in 1851 and was intended for prisoners serving short sentences. Wandsworth, like many of the new prisons which the government built after 1840, contained children as well as adults. A month's hard labour in Wandsworth must have been a terrible experience for a twelve-year-old boy. John would have spent many hours each day 'picking oakum' – separating the fibres of tarry old rope. His hands would soon have become raw. Much of John's time would have been spent alone in a tiny cell where he was supposed to think about the crime he had committed. If he had misbehaved in any way during his month in prison, he would have been severely beaten with a birch rod.

The Enquiry

John Hearn was a victim of the revolution in punishment which occurred in Britain during the nineteenth century. Between 1842 and 1877, ninety new prisons were built across the country. Many of these prisons are still in use today and the prison sentence is still at the core of Britain's punishment system. The massive prison building programme after 1842 was one response to people's concerns about the increase in crime during the first half of the nineteenth century. Another response to the rising crime rate was the formation of Britain's first professional police force. It was during the nineteenth century that the police force we know today was created. These changes marked a clear break with the past and were the beginning of the system of law and order which still operates in Britain.

This enquiry will focus on the three big changes in crime and punishment in the period 1750–1900:

1. changes in the crime rate and in the nature of crime
2. changes in law enforcement
3. changes in punishments, particularly the growth of prisons.

Your challenge is to describe these changes and to explain why each occurred at that time. As you find out about the changes you will collect information and ideas on three annotated timelines.

As in the previous two enquiries, it will be useful to begin with an overview of some of the big changes in Britain during this period …

Britain 1750–1900: an overview

1. Industrialisation

In the hundred years after 1750, something extraordinary happened
in Britain – the Industrial Revolution. For centuries, British people had
lived in villages and small towns, making everything they needed by
hand. Then, between 1750 and 1850, Britain became the world's first
industrial country. New methods of iron production were developed.
Coal was mined on a huge scale. New spinning and weaving machines
were invented which transformed the production of textiles. In the
north of England, industrialists built enormous wool and cotton
factories. In the period 1750–1900, industrialisation and the growth
of trade meant that Britain became the world's wealthiest nation.

◀ A steam-powered cotton mill in Manchester, 1835

2. Urbanisation

After 1750, Britain's population rocketed. From
around 6 million in 1750, it grew to 21 million in
1850, and to 37 million by 1900. There was
also a massive movement of population
from rural areas to towns and cities. In
1750, London was the only great city
in Britain, but by the middle of the
nineteenth century huge industrial
cities such as Manchester,
Birmingham, Leeds and Bradford
had emerged. People poured
into the cities to work in the new
factories. By 1850, for the first
time in Britain's history, more
people lived in towns and cities
than in rural areas. For the majority
of people, the villages and small towns
where everyone knew each other were
a thing of the past.

▼ Bradford, a new
industrial city, 1873

3. Class divisions

Industrialisation brought wealth to some people in Britain, but poverty to others. There was a wide gulf between the lives of rich and poor. In the nineteenth century, the upper and middle classes moved out of the centres of industrial towns and cities. They built large villas in the suburbs and countryside. Working-class people often lived in overcrowded terraced houses close to the factories where many of them worked. The wealthy and the poor led separate lives, but nearly all upper and middle-class families employed servants to work in their houses. Rich and poor people also encountered each other in the town centres where the wealthy went to shop.

◀ 'Poverty and Wealth' by William Powell Frith, 1888

4. Urban poverty

Life for the labouring poor in Britain's towns and cities could be very grim. All large towns in early industrial Britain had lodging houses where single people lived, and where newly-arrived families sometimes stayed while they looked for a house to rent. Lodging houses were often full of strangers living to together in filthy, overcrowded conditions. Many settled families lived in small back-to-back houses. These were often built around courts or yards, entered through a narrow alley from a main street. The families of poor labourers who became unemployed faced particular hardship. In the period 1750–1900, the government did not provide any benefit to people seeking work and it could therefore be a struggle for people to survive.

▼ A photograph of a Manchester yard, 1896

5. Rural poverty

The families of rural labourers continued to live in poverty throughout the period 1750–1900. A poor labourer often struggled to provided enough food for his children. George Mitchell, who was brought up in a labouring family in Somerset during the 1830s, was sometimes so hungry that he ate turnips from the fields and collected snails to roast for his tea. A slump in agriculture during the 1870s and 1880s made this a time of particular hardship for rural families. Many unemployed rural workers had to walk long distances seeking work.

▲ 'Hard Times', a painting by Sir Hubert von Herkomer, 1885

6. Changing beliefs

Between 1680 and 1830, philosophers and scientists in Britain, Europe and America began to think in different ways about what it means to be human. They wrote essays and books which led to fundamental changes in people's beliefs and attitudes. Historians call this period 'The Enlightenment'. The Enlightenment thinkers shared the common belief that traditional ways of doing things should be questioned. One man who took these ideas forward in the nineteenth century was Jeremy Bentham. Bentham proposed many legal and social reforms. He developed the philosophy of utilitarianism based on 'the greatest happiness for the greatest number'. When he died he had his body preserved and displayed in a wooden case. As you can see, the mummification of his head didn't go too well so they used a wax version instead.

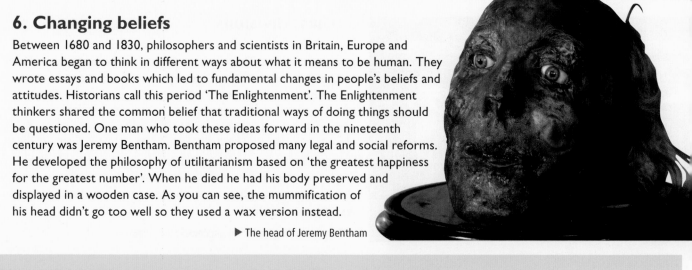

▶ The head of Jeremy Bentham

7. The British Empire

In 1750, Britain was already an important trading nation with colonies in America and the West Indies. The American colonies became independent in 1783, but Britain's Empire continued to grow in other parts of the world. At the end of the eighteenth century, Britain fought a war with France and gained control of much of India. In 1770, James Cook charted the east coast of Australia. Thirteen years later the government put forward a proposal to establish a settlement in New South Wales, and the British colonisation of Australia began. This map shows the extent of the British Empire in 1886 (Britain's territories are coloured pink). By the end of the nineteenth century much of Africa was also under British control. In 1900, Britain ruled one fifth of the world's land and a quarter of the world's population.

◀ A map of the British Empire in 1886

8. Railways

The first inter-city railway in the world opened between Liverpool and Manchester in 1830. During the 1830s and 1840s, a network of railways was built across much of Britain. The work of blasting the tunnels, laying the lines and moving the earth was done by navvies – workers from Ireland and rural parts of Britain who lived tough lives in temporary camps along the line. By 1850, most major towns were connected by rail. The age of the stagecoach came to an end as people and goods were increasingly transported by train. Some middle-class people who bought shares in the new railways made a lot of money from their investments. But not all owners of railway companies were honest men.

▼ The Liverpool and Manchester Railway, 1830

9. Growing literacy

In the late eighteenth century, charities and churches began to provide schools for poorer children. During the nineteenth century, the government also began to get involved in education. In 1870, an Education Act provided schools for all children under the age of ten. Improvements in education meant that more people could read and this fuelled a growth in demand for newspapers. Daily and weekly newspapers began to play an important part in people's lives as more and more people enjoyed reading about sporting events, politics and crimes. The weekly *Illustrated Police News*, first published in 1864, contained sensational stories of murders and hangings. It was enjoyed by many working-class readers.

▶ The Illustrated Police News, 1867

10. The growth of democracy

Until 1832, only 5 per cent of the population could vote in elections for the House of Commons and no women were allowed to vote. Few of Britain's new industrial cities were represented by their own Member of Parliament (MP). In the early nineteenth century, some people began to campaign for 'parliamentary reform'. Change came with the 1832 Reform Act which gave the vote to middle-class men and allowed the larger towns to have two MPs each. In 1867 and 1884, the vote was extended to working-class men, but women were still not allowed to vote. During the nineteenth century, national and local government became more involved in changing and reforming life in Britain.

◀ A debate in the House of Commons, 1887

11. Alcohol

During the nineteenth century, pubs played a major part in the lives of many labouring people. The pub provided a warm, well-lit and pleasant escape from the slums. Some poorer people became addicted to alcohol and drank huge quantities of beer and whisky. Gin, too, remained a problem, even after the end of the 'gin craze' in 1751. Drunkenness led to violence and caused misery in many working-class families. It became such an issue in the nineteenth century that a 'Temperance Movement' was formed which tried to persuade people to stop drinking alcohol. It had limited success.

▶ A crowded pub in the East End of London, 1871

Crimes and criminals, 1750–1900

Record

As you find out about crime and criminals, collect information and ideas on an annotated timeline like this one:

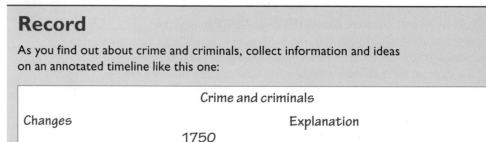

The economic and social changes caused by the Industrial Revolution had an enormous impact on crime, particularly theft. Factories, warehouses and shops were full of goods which could be stolen. In the industrial period, theft from the workplace became a much more common crime. Hundreds of new banks opened in towns and cities across Britain, and bank robbery increased. The homes of the middle classes, stuffed with possessions, were tempting targets for burglars. In these ways, industrial Britain provided many new opportunities for thieves.

The changing economic and social conditions also led to totally new crimes. Fare-dodging or vandalism on the new railways, stealing water from standpipes owned by water companies and failing to send your children to school (after 1870) were all unknown crimes in 1750. The growth of business created new opportunities for 'white-collar crime'. Corrupt bankers and businessmen sometimes embezzled their investors. In the 1840s, George Hudson, the 'railway king', swindled middle-class shareholders out of huge sums of money. These new crimes partly contributed to the overall increase in crime during the period 1750–1850.

Features of crime, 1750–1900

As you know, it is not easy for historians to measure changes in the crime rate. There are no national crime figures before 1805. Factors such as the new opportunities for crime, the number of unreported crimes and the impact of crackdowns on particular crimes, make it difficult to be precise about changes in the crime rate. However, historians are certain about the main features of crime in the period 1750–1900:

1. In the second half of the eighteenth century, there was a gradual increase in crime. This was followed by a very sharp increase in the crime rate after 1815. Crime then continued to rise until 1850, but more slowly. During the second half of the nineteenth century, there was a gradual fall in the crime rate.

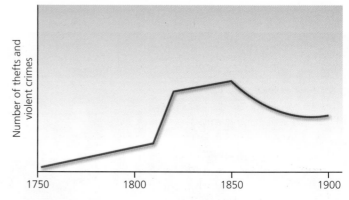

▲ Graph showing trends in the crime rate, 1750–1900

2. The most common form of crime was petty theft. The theft of low-value items and small amounts of money accounted for well over half of all crime, and sometimes as much as 80 per cent.

3. Violent crime was rare. Only 10 per cent of crimes involved violence. The murder rate was low. Usually, the murderer and the murder victim were members of the same family, or at least knew each other.

4. There were some 'professional' criminals who planned burglaries and who committed more than one offence. However, most crime was opportunistic (unplanned) and was committed by first-time offenders. These offenders were usually poor people who stole from shops, market stalls or their workplace. They were often driven to crime through desperation.

5. About three in four of all offenders were male. These were usually young men in their teens and early twenties. Women were rarely involved in crime. The most common offence for which women were charged was prostitution.

Reflect

Which of these features of crime in the period 1750–1900 were similar to the Middle Ages and the early modern period? Which are similar to today?

Causes of the increase in crime in the early nineteenth century

The rise in crime in the first half of the nineteenth can be partly explained by the increase in population. The rapid rise in population after 1750 meant that there were many more offenders and potential victims. Another factor contributing to the rise in crime was the growth of industry and trade. This meant that there were more goods for people to steal. The environment of the growing towns and cities also helped to create the conditions for increased criminal activity. The city centre, which attracted crowds of people to its shops and pubs, was often the scene of thefts and assaults. In the overcrowded lodging houses, packed with poor migrants, people's possessions could easily be stolen. The crowded courts and alleyways of poor urban neighbourhoods were difficult to police and could hide all kinds of criminal activity.

Population growth, industrialisation and the nature of city life are all underlying causes of the increase in crime across the period 1750–1850, but they cannot explain why there should be such big fluctuations in the crime rate. Poverty, and the distress which poor people faced during periods of high unemployment, are crucial factors in explaining particularly steep rises in crime.

▲ 'The Picadilly Nuisance' by George Cruikshank, 1818

The graph below reveals a massive increase in crime after 1815. In that year, the Napoleonic Wars came to an end and thousands of soldiers returned to Britain looking for work. Most were disappointed. The wartime boom in agriculture had ended, and industries which had benefited from wartime production now began to lay off workers. Between 1815 and 1822, wages fell by about a third. The rising price of bread also added to the distress of labouring families. As the economic recession deepened, many poor parents struggled to feed their children. In desperation, some turned to theft. The confessions of poor offenders when they appeared in court suggest that economic hardship was often the immediate cause of crime.

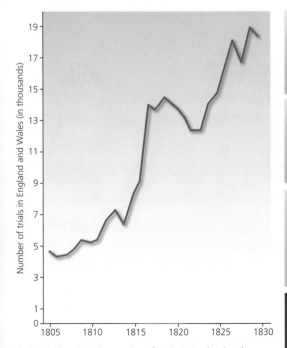

▲ Graph showing the number of trials in England and Wales (in thousands), 1805–30

William Dennison, a sixteen-year-old from London, admitted stealing a coat in 1816

I do not wish to add falsehood to fraud, I own (admit) I took the coat, but it was from mere distress.

Thomas Parkins, from a village in Bedfordshire, was prosecuted for stealing two faggots (bundles of sticks) from a local landowner in 1819

I was in great distress, my wife near lying in (having a baby), I went to get a faggot, to make her a bit of fire.

John Stone, of Leicester, was prosecuted for stealing a watch in 1822

I am a poor stocking weaver in distress. I was travelling into Leicestershire, after having been to London to offer myself for a soldier; but was not tall enough. My parents are in distress, my father out of employment. I have eight brothers and sisters …

Reflect

What can these confessions tell us about the reasons why individuals committed theft in the early nineteenth century?

Nineteenth-century views and attitudes

As the crime rate rocketed in the early nineteenth century, people became increasingly concerned. In letters, books, reports and newspapers, writers expressed a range of views about criminals and the rise in crime. Many were particularly concerned about juvenile crime and the growing number of young offenders. Some 'radical thinkers' made the link between poverty and crime. They argued that the poor environment in which many working-class children grew up was, in fact, the main cause of crime.

They often placed an emphasis on the lack of education, religion and useful work.

John Glyde is a good example of a radical thinker who was concerned about crime. Glyde was born into an ordinary working family in Suffolk in 1824, but he educated himself and wrote many books about the county. In 1850, he published *The Moral, Social and Religious Condition of Ipswich in the Middle of the Nineteenth Century*, which included these thoughts on crime.

Over the last fifty years there has been a great change in the offences committed in the borough. From offences against the person it has changed to offences against property. The number of offences has alarmingly increased since the great influx of population …

The amount of juvenile delinquency is a branch of the criminal question especially worthy of our consideration … In 1849 there were 26 juveniles in prison and the length of time each was confined averaged four weeks. The total cost for the maintenance of the 26 juveniles while in prison was £74 12s 3d.

Their education is very defective, one third of them can neither read nor write … 'Ragged schools' have been instituted; and if these are combined with an industrial school, much good will be effected.

It is to our low neighbourhoods, and to neglected children roaming the streets, that we must look if we would check the current of crime. It is to these districts that attention must be turned, to nip the evil in the bud.

Reflect

What do these extracts from John Glyde's book reveal about his concerns?

Many middle-class people in nineteenth-century Britain held more conservative views about crime and criminals than John Glyde and other radicals. They often blamed the spread of crime on the bad moral habits of the poor, the worst of these being drunkenness. These people thought that alcohol was the main reason for the increase in crime. They were dismayed by the growing number of beer houses and the misery which drunkenness brought to many families. A growing number of people joined the Temperance Movement which argued that the public house left the poor without money for food and led to gambling, prostitution and violence.

▼ An engraving of a public house, 1879

There were plenty of people in nineteenth-century Britain who took a harsh view of criminals. In their opinion, poor people made a deliberate choice to become criminals instead of working. Some writers argued that there was a particular group of poor people who could be described as the 'criminal class' and that children born into this class inherited criminal tendencies from their parents. Others argued that that there was a 'criminal type' and that this was reflected in the appearance of criminals. They quoted the work of some medical scientists who claimed criminals could be identified by their physical features – the shape of the skull or of the hands. The photographs of prisoners which were taken in many gaols after 1850 were intended not only to identify prisoners, but also to support these theories about the physical appearance of prisoners.

Reflect

Why do you think each of the photographs included the hands of the prisoners?

▲ Photographs of prisoners in Dorchester Gaol, 1870s

People in nineteenth-century Britain were very interested in crime, particularly the details of murders and murderers. When Madam Tussaud's waxworks opened in 1802, people were particularly keen to see the models of murderers. They enjoyed the novels of Charles Dickens which contained detailed descriptions of London's criminals. Most of all, they bought the 'penny dreadfuls' – cheap illustrated weekly newspapers which gave detailed reports of the most shocking crimes. These newspapers often contained graphic illustrations of murders which it would be illegal to print today. Some middle-class campaigners felt that such publications corrupted the minds of young people and created an unhealthy interest in crime.

Reflect

Which of the nineteenth-century views and attitudes discussed on these pages are still common today?

▶ The front page of *The Illustrated Police News*, 8 September 1888

Changes in law enforcement, 1750–1900

▲ A photograph of police officers at Rose Hill police station, Liverpool, in 1900

Reflect

What do you find interesting about this photograph?

This photograph from 1900 shows the police officers at Rose Hill police station in Liverpool. Rose Hill was just one of several police stations which had opened in Liverpool after 1836. The men look very different from the police officers we would find in Liverpool today, but we can recognise them as part of a 'modern' police force.

Between 1750 and 1900, there was a remarkable change in policing in Britain. In 1750, some towns employed watchmen to patrol the streets, but the law was mainly enforced by unpaid parish constables and other office-holders working in their spare time. By 1900, every town and county had a professional, uniformed and full-time police force. Across Britain, policemen prevented crime by patrolling particular streets known as their 'beat'. This huge change in policing did not happen easily. As you will discover, there was much opposition to the introduction of police forces in Britain

Record

As you find out about the development of law enforcement, produce your second annotated timeline.

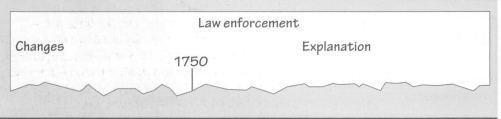

Policing in 1750

In 1750, law enforcement was still based on medieval and early modern methods of policing. Parish constables were selected or volunteered to serve as part-time and unpaid law-enforcers for a limited time. Constables could arrest offenders, but no one expected them to prevent crime by patrolling the parish. Some towns employed watchmen to patrol the streets after dark, or paid 'thief-takers' to catch thieves, but these methods had limited success in reducing urban crime.

In the later eighteenth century, the limitations of policing became clear, particularly in the towns where rapid population growth led to big increases in crime. London, with its huge migrant population, great wealth and terrible poverty, faced serious challenges. It is not surprising, therefore, that the first moves towards more professional policing took place in the capital.

The Bow Street Runners, 1750s

The man who led the way was Sir John Fielding. In 1754, Fielding took over as magistrate at Bow Street Court in central London, and served there until 1780. In the 1750s, Fielding organised groups of part-time constables who were paid to patrol London's main streets and roads each evening until midnight. Bow Street Court began to resemble a police station. The constables became known as the 'Bow Street Runners'. By 1800, 68 men formed the Bow Street Patrol.

In 1773, John Fielding made another contribution to the development of policing by publishing information about crime. Magistrates from all over the country sent details of criminals and stolen property to Bow Street and these were published in a weekly newspaper, *The Hue and Cry*. Fielding even managed to persuade the government to back the newspaper by providing £400 a year.

After 1775, John Fielding put forward more plans for preventing crime in London and across Britain. These included extending his system of paid constables to towns and rural areas all over the country. Fielding's ideas for developing police forces were radical and would have cost money. For these reasons, they were not supported during his lifetime. But John Fielding's work was important in changing people's ideas and attitudes in the years after 1780.

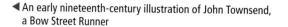
◀ An early nineteenth-century illustration of John Townsend, a Bow Street Runner

▲ A portrait of Sir John Fielding, by Nathaniel Hone, 1762

▲ A portrait of Sir Robert Peel, c. 1846

Robert Peel and the beginning of the Metropolitan Police Force, 1829

At the beginning of the nineteenth century, London's Bow Street Runners, constables and watchmen were struggling to enforce law and order in the city. Crime was rising and the government feared that protests about unemployment, high food prices and the unfair political system could turn into a revolution.

Yet many people were opposed to idea of a centralised London police force paid for by the government:

- They thought it would cost too much.
- They did not think it was the job of government to set up and control a police force.
- They feared that a large force, which might be armed, could be used by the government to brutally suppress all protest.

In 1822, when Robert Peel became Home Secretary he was determined to overcome this opposition and to deal with London's policing problems. Peel was a skilful politician and administrator. By 1829, he had won support in parliament for the setting up of the Metropolitan Police. London was now policed by a force of 3,000 men paid for by the government out of taxes. The 'Met' was led by two police commissioners at Scotland Yard who reported directly to the Secretary of State. With the creation of the Metropolitan Police in 1829, the age of 'modern' policing had begun.

▶ A photograph of a 'Peeler'

Officers in the Metropolitan Police were soon nicknamed 'peelers' or 'bobbies'. To ensure that they did not look like soldiers, police officers wore a dark blue tall hat and coat. They were unarmed, apart from a truncheon. At first, there was much opposition to the new force, but gradually people began to accept this new method of policing.

Developments in policing after 1829

The changes in policing which Peel introduced applied only to London but, from the 1830s, the government passed three laws which led to the spread of separate, locally-controlled police forces all across Britain:

1835 Municipal Corporations Act
This allowed towns across the country to set up a police force. Of the 178 towns mentioned in the Act, only 100 had a police force by the beginning of 1838, and many of these were quite small. Attitudes were often slow to change because of money. The police forces were under local control and were paid for by local rates. Many ratepayers were concerned about the cost.

1839 Rural Constabulary Act
The Act allowed magistrates to establish a police force for their county. After 1839, some counties set up a professional police force paid for by local rates. But progress was slow, often because of cost. By 1855, only two-thirds of counties had a police force.

1856 The County and Borough Police Act
The local police forces which had been set up in the two decades after 1835 were under local control. The government wanted to create a national system of policing and the 1856 Act was a first step towards this. Three new Inspectors of Constabulary ensured that local forces met national standards. The government provided a quarter of the funding for forces which the inspectors decided were efficient. In 1876, this funding was extended to half.

The changing role of police officers after 1850

The role of police officers in the second half of the nineteenth century was varied. A big part of their job was clamping down on behaviour which middle-class people found offensive. They removed drunks, prostitutes and vagrants from the streets. In some areas, they cracked down heavily on public houses which allowed Sunday drinking, gambling and illegal sports. But the prevention of theft and violence was the main function of the police. It is difficult to be certain about their success, but it is likely that the new police forces made a big contribution to the fall in crime in the second half of the nineteenth century.

The most important role of the new police was in preventing crime. It was still down to individual people to bring prosecutions, but the police were drawn into being prosecutors if the victim was too poor to bring a prosecution.

If uniformed police officers on the beat became increasingly effective at preventing crime, catching criminals was another matter. Big changes in crime detection would not occur until the twentieth century,

but there were some important developments in the last part of the nineteenth century. Detectives were first used by the Metropolitan Police in 1842. This was developed in 1878 when the Criminal Investigation Department (CID) was set up at Scotland Yard. By the mid-1880s, 800 men worked in the CID and it had become an important part of the police service.

At first, the work of the new detectives was limited. They interviewed witnesses and used clues from the crime scene. Often the most helpful clue was a footprint which they could match to a suspect's shoe. But before the end of the nineteenth century new forms of technology began to be used in crime detection:

- From the 1880s, detectives began to take photographs of crime scenes.
- In 1867, the telegraph was first used to speed up police communication.
- In 1897, fingerprinting began to be used in British India. Fingerprinting would become a crucial method of crime detection in the twentieth century.

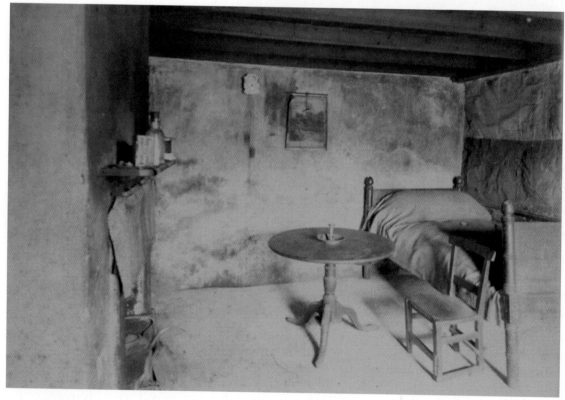

◀ A police photograph of the scene of a murder in Jersey, 1894

The courts

Compared with the huge changes in policing, the developments in the system of courts were quite small in the period 1750–1900. Felons continued to be tried at the assizes and quarter sessions. During the nineteenth century, it became more common at a trial for lawyers to act for the prosecution and for the defence. Trials became longer and more formal. People who had committed minor offences continued to appear in front of magistrates at the petty sessions.

Changes in punishment, 1750–1900

In 1879 the woman in this picture, Kate Webster, was hanged at Wandsworth Gaol. She had been found guilty of murdering her employer, Julia Martha Thompson. The case was particularly gruesome and attracted lots of public interest. The Illustrated Police News produced a special souvenir edition about the crime, trial and execution of Kate Webster.

◀ An illustration of the execution of Kate Webster in the *Illustrated Police News*, July 1879

Reflect

What interesting details of the execution can you see in the picture?

Kate was a 30-year-old Irishwoman who had migrated to England in her early twenties. She had served several prison sentences for theft. In March 1879 she began working as a maid for Mrs Thompson, a former schoolteacher who lived in Richmond, London. Their relationship quickly soured. On 2 March Kate Webster murdered Mrs Thompson by throwing her down the stairs and then strangling her. She disposed of the body by cutting it into pieces, burying the head and placing some of the remains in a box which she threw into the River Thames.

The discovery of the box led to her arrest, trial and death sentence.

The execution of Kate Webster took place inside Wandsworth Gaol at 9.00 am on Tuesday 29 July. The hangman, William Marwood, used his newly-developed 'long drop' technique. When the trapdoor was released, her body dropped eight feet causing instant death. At 9.05 am a black flag was raised over the prison to show that the death sentence had been carried out. The large crowd of people who had gathered outside Wandsworth Gaol gave a loud cheer.

By the time of Kate Webster's execution, the punishment of criminals in Britain had changed a lot since 1750. Between 1750 and 1900 there were important developments, not only in capital punishment, but also in transportation and prisons.

Record

As you find out about the development of punishments you should produce your third and final annotated timeline: **Changes in Punishment, 1750–1900**

- On the left of your timeline add points to describe changes in punishments which took place
- On the right of your timeline add points to explain why punishments changed, and to summarize the people's attitudes towards punishment.

Use different colours for capital punishment, transportation and prisons.

Changes in capital punishment

The 'new drop'

From the late eighteenth century, attitudes towards capital punishment began to change. In the 1780s, the government became increasingly concerned about rowdy behaviour of the lower classes on 'hanging days' and encouraged magistrates to move executions behind the prison walls. At the same time, a more humane form of hanging known as the 'new drop' was introduced. This allowed the condemned person to fall through a trap door and therefore to die more quickly.

More and more 'new drops' were constructed at county gaols. Often the 'new drop gallows' were set up on the flat roof of the prison gatehouse where people could get a view. In the early-nineteenth century, executions were still public, but the days of the long cart ride to the gallows, the jeering crowds and the slow strangulation came to an end.

Reflect

The government still wanted the public to witness executions even after they moved them behind prison walls. Why do you think this was?

Fewer executions

From the beginning of the nineteenth century, there was also a big reduction in the number of executions. In the decade 1800–1809, 871 people suffered the death penalty in England and Wales. By 1830–1839 the number had fallen to 297. Many people, influenced by the humanitarian values which came from the Enlightenment, began to think that execution for minor crimes was morally wrong.

Over the period 1832 to 1837, Sir Robert Peel's government removed a number of crimes from the list of capital offences. These included:

- Sheep, cattle and horse stealing (1832)
- Letter stealing (1834)
- Forgery and coining (1836)
- Arson, burglary and theft from a house (1837)

After 1837 the only hanging crimes were murder and attempted murder. In 1868 the government took the further step of making public executions illegal. After 1868 murderers like Kate Webster were hanged out of sight, behind prison walls.

The 'long drop'

In the late nineteenth century, the method of hanging also became more humane. In 1872, William Marwood, developed the technique of the 'long drop'. This calculated exactly how much rope an individual needed to break the neck instantly. In 1874 Marwood used the technique when he became executioner for London and Middlesex. It was thanks to him that Kate Webster had a quick and painless death. During the 1870s, the 'long drop' was gradually introduced by gaols across Britain.

Record

Start your final timeline. Explain the changes in capital punishment.

Transportation

In 1750, people whose crimes did not deserve the death penalty were transported to Britain's colonies in America where they were forced to work on plantations. Transportation to America had been used as a punishment since the end of the seventeenth century, but it would soon end. In 1776, America declared its independence from Britain, making transportation across the Atlantic impossible. At first, the government's solution was to imprison people on 'hulks' – old, rotting warships situated on the River Thames. Conditions on the overcrowded and filthy 'hulks' were terrible. For much of the time prisoners were kept in irons. Many died of diseases such dysentery and typhus.

During the 1780s, the government desperately needed to find another place which could be used for transportation. It finally decided to send convicts to south-eastern Australia. In 1770, this territory had been mapped and claimed for Britain by Captain Cook. From the government's perspective, transportation to Australia had several advantages:

● Australia was an unknown place on the other side of the world. The thought of being transported there might deter potential criminals.
● Removing criminals enabled the government to get rid of people from the 'criminal classes' and would therefore reduce crime.
● The convicts would provide the labour needed to build Britain's new territory in Australia.

In May 1787, the first fleet of eleven ships, carrying 736 convicts, set off for Australia. Eight months later they arrived in Botany Bay. Forty-eight convicts had died on the journey. Between 1787 and 1868, around 160,000 convicts were transported to Australia. Transportation reached a peak in the 1830s when 5,000 people a year were sent to the convict colony in Australia.

▼ An engraving of a convict hulk at Portsmouth, 1828

The convict colony

Around 80 per cent of convicts had stolen food, clothing or items of small value. The average age of prisoners was 26, but some were very young. James Grace, who sailed in the first fleet, and whose crime was stealing some ribbon and a pair of silk stockings, was just eleven years old. Some of those transported were political prisoners who had been involved in protests. The most famous of these were the Tolpuddle Martyrs, sentenced to seven years' transportation in 1834 for trying to form a trades union.

All convicts transported to Australia faced seven years, fourteen years, or a lifetime of hard labour. They worked in gangs digging ditches, felling trees, planting crops, putting up buildings and constructing roads. Often they worked with heavy iron chains around their ankles. At night they were locked up in convict barracks. Road-building gangs slept in prison huts on wheels which they dragged behind them as the road was made. Britain's penal colony in Australia was based on harsh punishment. Convicts who broke the rules were given 25, 50 or as many as 100 lashes. Some convicts tried to escape but few survived for very long in the harsh environment of the Australian bush. Prisoners who had served their sentence usually worked for one of the free settlers. Few could ever afford the cost of the journey to return home.

▲ An engraving of a convict being flogged, 1836

By the 1830s, people were beginning to criticise the use of transportation as a punishment. Humanitarians argued that conditions on the convict ships and in the penal colony were cruel and inhumane. Ratepayers complained that they had to support the families of men who were transported. Some people argued that transportation was a 'soft option', as it gave released prisoners the chance to start a new life in Australia. The government also came under pressure from the authorities in Australia who objected to the 'dumping' of convicts in their country. In the period from 1830–60, a number of Select Committees of the House of Commons heard many people argue against transportation. From the 1840s onwards, fewer convicts were transported, and in 1868, the government ended transportation completely.

Record

In a different colour, add points to your timeline to explain changes in transportation.

Prisons

In the period 1750–1900, the punishment of offenders changed dramatically. As hangings began to decline after 1800, and as fewer convicts were transported after 1840, the prison sentence became the most important form of punishment. It was in the nineteenth century that our modern punishment system, with imprisonment at its core, began.

Record

Add this important point to your timeline.

In 1750, prisons were grim places. Gaolers often ran prisons as businesses. Prisoners with money were expected to pay for everything – bedding, candles, coal, a table, food. Poorer prisoners depended on local charities, or went without. Over half of all prisoners were debtors. Others had served their sentence but were still in prison because they could not afford the discharge fee demanded by the gaoler. Few gaolers attempted to give prisoners anything useful to do. Some inflicted brutal punishments on prisoners such as whipping or placing them in irons. Prisons in 1750 were often overcrowded, damp and insanitary places. Many inmates died of 'gaol fever' (typhus) and other diseases.

In the period after 1770, some people began to campaign for the reform (improvement) of prisons. These individuals were often motivated by humanitarian and religious beliefs. The prison reformers felt that prisoners should be able to live in safety and dignity. They argued that prisoners should be helped to change their ways and to become good citizens. Two prison reformers are particularly remembered today: John Howard and Elizabeth Fry.

◄ A statue of John Howard in St Paul's Cathedral, 1795

John Howard

When John Howard became High Sherriff of Bedfordshire in 1773 he was shocked by the state of the county gaol. Howard visited other prisons and found that conditions were just as bad. In 1774, he gave evidence at the House of Commons to support two new laws:

- **The Discharged Prisoners Act** abolished the discharge fees which prisoners were expected to pay before they were released.
- **The Health of Prisoners Act** ordered that prisons should be regularly cleaned and whitewashed. Baths were to be introduced into all prisons and separate rooms were to be provided for sick prisoners.

John Howard was not content with these changes. He continued to travel in England, Ireland and Europe, making careful studies of the condition in different prisons. In 1777, he published his great work, *The State of the Prisons*. This was the first detailed study of the country's prisons. *The State of the Prisons* recommended that:

- Prisons should be built near a supply of clean water.
- Gaolers should live in the prison and should be paid a salary.
- Different categories of prisoner should have their own blocks and yards.
- Each prisoner should have their own sleeping cell.
- Prisoners should have adequate food and clean shirts twice a week.

When John Howard died in 1790, the government had still not enforced these reforms by law, but some High Sheriffs began to build new gaols based on his ideas in the period 1780–1820.

▲ An 1863 engraving of Elizabeth Fry reading to the women prisoners in Newgate prison in 1816

Elizabeth Fry

Elizabeth Gurney was born into a Quaker family in Norwich. In 1800, she married the wealthy Quaker Joseph Fry, and the couple settled in London. In 1813, Elizabeth Fry visited the women's section of Newgate prison and was shocked by what she saw. Three hundred women were crammed into a space designed for 50. Some had no money to pay for bedding. Others were ill and could not afford a doctor. Elizabeth Fry was horrified that so many children and babies lived with their mothers in these conditions.

As a Quaker, Elizabeth Fry believed that there is something of God in everyone, and that prisoners should be encouraged to live decent lives. She was determined to improve the conditions for the women in Newgate gaol. By 1816, she had established a small school in the women's section of the prison where she and her Quaker friends read to the prisoners.

But the school was just the beginning of Elizabeth Fry's reforms at Newgate. She persuaded the prison authorities to divide the women into groups of twelve according their age and offence. Each group was supervised by a matron who encouraged the women to read from the Bible. The women were given materials for sewing and knitting. The selling of alcohol was banned on the women's side of the prison. Elizabeth Fry's focus was on reforming conditions in just one prison, but in speaking and writing about the reforms at Newgate she had a much wider influence.

Reflect

In what ways did the work of John Howard and Elizabeth Fry differ?

Changing prisons, 1800–1900

In 1811, the government began the construction of a new national prison which would reform prisoners by enforcing religious, silent reflection and work. The site chosen for the prison was Millbank, on the north bank of the River Thames, only half a mile away from the Houses of Parliament. Millbank Penitentiary was a disaster. During its construction, the boggy land on which it was built caused huge cracks to appear in the building. When Millbank finally opened in 1816 it had cost the massive sum of £450,000. Discipline was a problem from the start. In February 1817, prisoners rioted, demanding an increase in their daily allowance of bread. The governor was sacked. The reputation of Millbank Penitentiary was in ruins.

▲ Millbank Penitentiary, drawn in 1829

The failure of Millbank may explain why the government did not try to build more prisons until 1842. Instead, it tried to reform the prison system by regulating local prisons. The **1823 Gaols Act** contained some important reforms:

- JPs had to visit their gaols and report on conditions.
- Each category of prisoner should have their own area in the prison.
- Women prisoners had to be supervised by female warders.
- Governors, surgeons and chaplains should visit prisoners regularly.
- Each prisoner should have a separate sleeping cell with a bed or a hammock.

All this cost money, and the Act was often ignored. Prison inspectors were not appointed until 1835 and they had limited powers.

In the 1840s, the decline of transportation led to a new wave of prison building. In 1842, the government opened Pentonville prison in London as a 'model' national prison. By 1850, 50 prisons had been built or re-built. By 1877, the number had reached 90. Pentonville and many other prisons operated the **separate system** which had been first used in America. Prisoners were kept in individual cells where they worked, prayed and reflected on their crimes. They left their cells only for services in the prison chapel and for exercise. Under this severe system, prisoners were driven to despair by the loneliness. Many suffered mental breakdown and some took their own life.

Reflect

Examine the two pictures carefully. How were prisoners prevented from speaking to each other in the chapel and the exercise yard?

◄ An 1862 engraving of prisoners exercising at Pentonville prison

▼ An 1862 engraving of prisoners in the chapel at Wandsworth prison

From the 1850s, some people began to think that changing prisoners was impossible and that punishment and deterrence were what prisons should be about. Some people were also concerned about the expense of the separate system which had to provide prisoners with individual cells. The solution was the **silent system**. Prisoners were allowed to work together, but in silence. They were given pointless work:

- The treadmill – prisoners walked on a huge wheel, simply to make it turn.
- The crank – prisoners turned a crank handle thousands of times a day. Warders could tighten the screws to make the crank harder to turn.
- Shot drill – prisoners moved heavy cannonballs from one side of a room to the other.

In the early 1860s, a number of people in London were choked and robbed on the streets. Newspaper reporting created 'garrotting panic' and politicians responded by making prisons even harsher. In 1863, they brought back flogging in prisons – it had only been abolished in 1861. The **1865 Prisons Act** emphasised 'hard labour, hard fare and hard board'. Strenuous, pointless work was increased, food was made deliberately monotonous and plank beds replaced hammocks. This brutal prison system remained in place for the next 30 years. It was the system which John Hearn – the twelve-year-old boy you met at the beginning of the enquiry – suffered in June 1873.

Record

Use a different colour to add changes in prisons to your punishments timeline.

Review

Use your punishment timeline to answer the following question:

How far do you agree that the work of prison reformers was the main reason for changes in prisons in the period 1750–1900?

The Ballad of Reading Gaol by Oscar Wilde

In the early 1890s, Oscar Wilde was one of London's most popular playwrights. He mixed with fashionable people and was much admired for his witty conversation and flamboyant dress. In 1891, Wilde had met Lord Alfred Douglas, the handsome but spoilt son of the Marquess of Queensbury. Oscar Wilde and Alfred Douglas became lovers, but Douglas's father was furious about their relationship. In 1895, Wilde was arrested and charged with 'gross indecency with men'. At that time gay sex was a crime in Britain, and would remain so until 1967. The court found Wilde guilty and sentenced him to two years' hard labour.

In May 1895, Oscar Wilde was imprisoned in London, first in Pentonville and then in Wandsworth. He was used to a comfortable life and the regime of 'hard labour, hard fare and hard bed' had a terrible effect on his health. In November, he collapsed in the chapel at Wandsworth from illness and hunger. Wilde spent two months in the prison infirmary and was then transferred to Reading gaol. He later described the humiliation he felt on the train journey as a crowd of people jeered and spat at him at Clapham station.

Reading gaol was built in 1844. From the outside it looked more like a castle than a prison, with its gatehouse, towers and high walls. The gaol had 250 cells divided into five wings spreading outwards from a central point. Oscar Wilde was taken to the top floor of C wing, cell 3. His cell was 13 feet long by 7 feet wide. It had a hammock, stool, table and some shelves. A gas light lit the notices on the cell walls: prison rules, details of Wilde's offences, morning and evening prayers. When the prison opened there had been a toilet in each cell, but this had been removed in the

▶ A photograph of Oscar Wilde, 1881

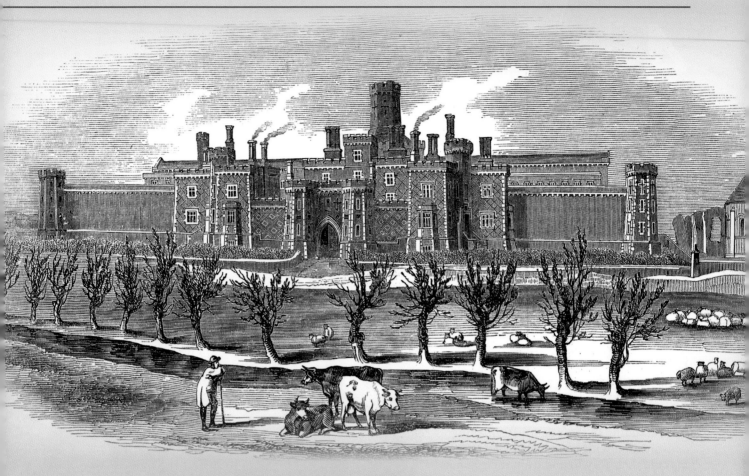

▲ An engraving of Reading gaol, 1844

1860s when the government made prisons harsher. Now, Wilde and the other prisoners had to 'slop out' their waste each morning, pouring the contents of their chamber pots into a central sluice.

The separate system was used at Reading gaol. Prisoners were kept alone in their cells nearly all the time. When Oscar Wilde and the other inmates went to chapel they wore a hood and sat in an individual cubicle so that the only person they could see was the chaplain. The separate system at Reading was enforced very harshly by the governor, Colonel Isaacson. Wilde later described him as having 'the eyes of a ferret, the body of an ape and the soul of a rat'. When one of the kinder warders, Tom Martin, gave biscuits to a poorly child prisoner, Isaacson had him sacked.

One Tuesday morning in July 1896, a prisoner in Reading gaol – a young soldier called Charles Wooldridge – was executed. At eight o'clock in the morning, he was taken to the 'Photographic House' between C and D wings. There, his legs and arms were tied with leather straps, a white hood was placed over his head, a noose was fixed around his neck and the trapdoor was released. Later that morning Charles Wooldridge was buried in an unmarked grave within the prison.

Wilde was deeply moved by the death of the young soldier. In 1898, after his release, Oscar Wilde wrote *The Ballad of Reading Gaol*. This long poem of 109 verses narrated the execution of Charles Wooldridge and highlighted the brutality of the prison system which all prisoners suffered.

In 1900, Oscar Wilde died in his room at a cheap hotel in Paris. These are three verses from his last work:

From *The Ballad of Reading Gaol*, by Oscar Wilde, 1898

We tore the tarry rope to shreds
With blunt and bleeding nails
We rubbed the doors, and scrubbed the floors
And cleaned the shining rails;
And, rank by rank, we soaped the plank
And clattered with the pails

Like ape or clown, in monstrous garb
With crooked arrows starred,
Silently we went round and round
The slippery asphalte yard;
Silently we went round and round
And no man spoke a word

This too I know – and wise it were
If each could know the same –
That every prison that men build
Is built with bricks of shame,
And bound with bars lest Christ should see
How men their brothers maim

4

Going nowhere?

Should we be encouraged by the story of crime and punishment since 1900?

In 1895, this picture appeared in an illustrated magazine called the Graphic. It shows a police constable struggling to arrest a member of one of the many gangs that operated in London's East End of London at that time. The artist has made the gang members look mean and rough as well as slightly comical. But an incident in the same area just two years later shows how gang violence was no laughing matter.

East London, 1897

In the early evening of Sunday 7 March 1897, pedestrians were milling around on Hackney Road, east London. Some were standing in their doorways making conversation with neighbours. Others were making their way to and from their homes or church services.

Suddenly the whole mood of the street changed as a crowd of about fifty or sixty youths came around the corner and marched menacingly up the road, yelling loudly. These were the Bethnal Green Boys, just one of the many violent gangs that operated in the area. They pushed anyone in their way from the pavements and confronted frightened locals, demanding to know where they could find any of the Broadway Boys, a Hackney-based rival gang.

Two police constables appeared at the bottom of the road, behind the youths. Before they reached the gang there was a bright flash and the sound of gunfire. When they saw a rival gang member, two youths pulled revolvers from their jackets and fired them into the air. One bullet smashed into the window of an ice cream parlour and others bounced off walls. Charles Luton, a boy of about eleven years of age, fell to the ground on a street corner. A stray bullet had embedded itself in his left knee.

As members of the public gathered around the injured boy, the gang split. As one group of youths ran down the side street they threw a glass bottle at the policeman chasing them. It missed him and shattered on the ground. He finally cornered the group and arrested them but only after one had thrown a revolver into a canal. The main group also ran away

▲ A gang member is arrested in London's East End, from *The Graphic* magazine, 1895

and dispersed. One woman who watched them race past her doorway was alarmed to find a revolver that had been dropped onto her windowsill, still warm. A neighbour passed it to one of the many constables who were by now on the scene. It was found to be of a type that was regularly sold at a nearby cattle market for about one shilling.

A month later, at the Old Bailey court in London, the two gunmen were each sentenced to six months of hard labour in prison. Their innocent young victim, Charles Luton, gave evidence against them. The court heard that he would probably be lame for the rest of his life.

76

Liverpool, 2007

At 7.30 in the evening of Friday 22 August, eleven-year-old Rhys Jones was making his way home. He had just been to football practice and was cutting across a car park outside a pub. He did not notice a youth dressed in a black hoodie and tracksuit standing nearby.

The youth had his arms stretched out in front of him. He was holding a handgun and was taking aim at a small group of teenagers standing by their bikes on the far side of the car park. He fired three shots. One struck Rhys in the neck. The youths all ran off, leaving Rhys unconscious on the ground. He died a few hours later in hospital.

It took police eight months to track down the gunman. He was a seventeen-year-old who had been trying to kill a member of a rival street gang. He and the friends who tried to help him escape were put on trial and the killer was sent to prison for a minimum of twenty-two years. After passing sentence, the judge said that the offence arose from 'stupid, brutal gang conflict'.

▲ Tributes being paid at the place where Rhys Jones was murdered

---

Reflect

There were 110 years between the two shootings described on these pages.

1. How similar are the two incidents?
2. Do these two accounts make you feel optimistic or pessimistic about the chances of improving law and order in the years ahead?

The Enquiry

This book is about change and continuity. In the three different periods covered so far, you will have found many examples of change alongside a great continuity in the lawlessness of society.

In this enquiry you must decide whether the way crime and punishment have developed since 1900 makes you optimistic for the future. Your final judgement about this must be based on the evidence. You may find that others in your class reach a very different conclusion even though they are considering the same evidence. That does not matter. What matters is that your view and theirs are both evidence-based and that you have considered all sides of the argument.

You will be finding evidence about:

1. crime and criminals 1900 to present
2. enforcing the law 1900 to present
3. punishment 1900 to present.

As you work through the enquiry, capture the evidence in three different tables like this:

Crime and criminals 1900 to present		
Reasons to be optimistic	Summary of key events and features	Reasons to be pessimistic

Before you start gathering your evidence in the table, you will, as usual, be learning about the wider changes in society in these years.

Record

The next four pages summarise different aspects of life in Britain, 1900–2000. Read through them quickly and make a list of at least six specific features that you think may have affected crime and punishment at that time. Collect and explain your ideas in a table like this:

Specific features of life at this time	How I think this may have affected crime and punishment

1. Cities and towns

This photograph was taken from a satellite passing over Britain one night in 2012. The street lights clearly show the built up areas. This is an urban society. By 2011, over 80 per cent of the population were living in cities and large towns. Farming is still an important occupation but machines do much of the work and very few people now live on the land.

Over the twentieth century, cities spread so far that some have become conurbations, merging with outlying towns. People living in these cities may work several miles from their home. The days when people knew their neighbours well are long gone. For much of the twentieth century, the rich and middle classes lived away from the city and travelled in to work from the suburbs. The poor usually occupied the old houses near the centre or large new estates often in blocks of high-rise flats.

▶ The British Isles at night, 2012

2. Work and wealth

Britain's economy struggled for much of the first half of the twentieth century. The First World War (1914–18) disrupted normal business and the 1920s and 1930s saw mass unemployment and many strikes. The Second World War (1939–45) also damaged Britain's economy but by the 1950s a recovery was under way.

In 1957, the Prime Minister, Harold Macmillan, said that the country was experiencing prosperity unknown in his lifetime or in the history of Britain and added that most people 'had never had it so good'.

Britain was becoming a consumer society. People with jobs made all sorts of consumer items such as cars, washing machines and televisions or they provided services such as accounting, tourism or entertainment. They used their wages to buy these goods and services. This created even more jobs. By 2000, many more people owned their own homes and filled them with belongings that made them comfortable. All this was fuelled by advertising that made people feel that they should own all sorts of goods that previous generations never had. Buying also became easier from the 1960s with the arrival of credit cards.

▼ A cartoonist's view of Harold Macmillan enjoying consumer goods, 1959

3. Religion and rights

In 1900, the majority of people in Britain still attended church and 55 per cent of children went to Sunday school. By 2000, although over 70 per cent of British people described themselves as Christian, fewer than 10 per cent attended church. In the twentieth century, Christians could and did still influence society by their actions as individuals but the Church as an organisation lost much of its authority over people's lives and the shaping of new laws.

In 1948, Britain signed up to the Declaration of Human Rights created by the United Nations. Since then minority groups have worked hard to ensure they do not suffer ill-treatment on account of gender, race, religion or sexual orientation.

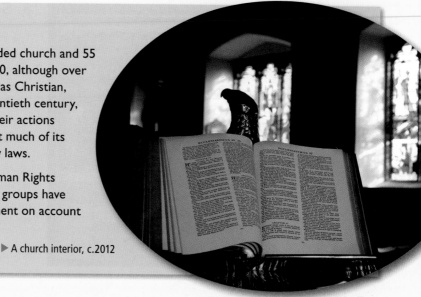

▶ A church interior, c.2012

4. Beliefs and attitudes

As fewer people relied on the Bible to explain human nature and human society, new approaches became popular in the twentieth century. Psychologists such as Sigmund Freud explained the human mind in ways that challenged what religious people called the 'soul'. Sociologists study societies and try to discover what shapes human behaviour. Some people have resisted these ways of explaining the world and say that they can lead to confusion over morality and a loss of a clear sense of what is right and wrong. Others say that past explanations have been little better than superstitious beliefs and that it is better to search for a scientifically based understanding of society.

◀ An artist's view of the human brain, c.2014

5. Government and control

From the 1880s, most working men over the age of 21 had the right to vote. Governments wanted to gain their support so they tried to help them. Between 1906 and 1911, the Liberal Party passed a series of laws that tried to tackle problems of poverty. This was the beginning of what we now call the 'Welfare State', where the government uses taxpayers' money to provide for the needs of the whole society, especially the poor and vulnerable.

By 1928, every adult in the country could vote and governments did more and more to provide for their needs in all areas of life. Politicians cared more about social issues that governments had previously paid little attention to. Governments are now far more directly involved in keeping people safe than they were before 1900. By 2010, the costs of the Welfare State and the degree of government involvement in people's lives seemed to have gone too far for many voters, and governments have tried to cut back on the costs while still promising to look after the people.

▶ The Houses of Parliament, Westminster, c.2010

79

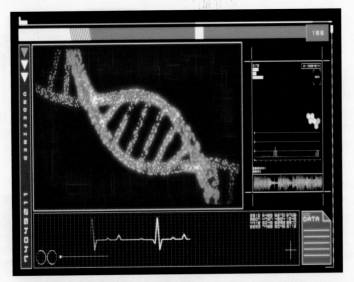

6. Science and technology

The twentieth century has seen the most extraordinary developments in science and technology. These have affected almost every aspect of our lives as this page in particular will show. Biological sciences have given the world antibiotics that end many infections that were once fatal. Surgeons working with sophisticated equipment can rescue lives that would certainly have been lost in past centuries. In the 1950s, scientists used X-rays to reveal the structure of the DNA, the building blocks of all life. By the 1950s, there was a safe supply of electricity to most homes in Britain and this has transformed the way we live and the gadgets that we use.

◀ A twenty-first century digital image of DNA

7. Transport and communication

In 1896, an Act of Parliament allowed the first motor cars on British roads, with a speed limit of 14 miles per hour. In 1919, the first regular aeroplane services carried passengers from London to Paris. Today, cars and aeroplanes allow people to travel further and more speedily than ever.

In 1901, the Italian inventor Marconi used enormous kites to lift radio aerials high in the sky and sent a wireless telegraph signal from America to England. The communication of people, images and ideas changed rapidly over the next century. By 1985, mobile telephones such as the one shown here were in use in Britain. They soon dropped in price and became much valued and extremely useful personal possessions that allowed anyone to contact someone else anywhere, at any time. At the same time, computers began to find a place in the home and in offices of all sorts – recording, sorting and sharing vast amounts of data at remarkable speed.

A Vodafone mobile telephone, 1985 ▶

8. Leisure and entertainment

In 1896, moving picture films were shown for the first time in Britain and cinemas were soon being built around the country. People complained that many adventure films set bad examples to young people. Television broadcasting began in the 1930s and by the 1970s over 90 per cent of homes had at least one set. Television helped to promote Britain's leading spectator sport, football, which drew massive crowds. Supporters travelled far and wide to watch their teams.

As Britain's wealth grew after 1960, most homes had radios and record players. These helped to develop Britain's popular music industry. Young people followed their favourite bands and enjoyed gathering at large and loud parties. For some this involved using music and parties to express their independence from their parents and from society's expectations. By 2010, the latest digital technology meant that music, as well as films, could be streamed or downloaded from the internet onto computers, tablets and mobile phones. Computer games became an enormous industry but, just like films in the early 1900s, some people complained that they encouraged unhealthy attitudes and behaviour.

◀ A twenty-first century computer game

9. Migration and diversity

Throughout the nineteenth century, immigrants moved to Britain, largely from Ireland but also from Germany and Italy. Around 1900, many thousands of Russian Jews arrived, seeking freedom from persecution. After the Second World War, Britain called for migrants to come and work in hospitals and in public transport. When Britain joined the European Union (EU) in 1973, it opened its doors to migrants from other member countries. The number who chose to move to Britain rose rapidly when many eastern European countries joined the EU in the 1990s.

In all these cases migrants have often had to live and work in the poorer areas of Britain's cities, at least in their first years in the country. Some local residents have found it difficult to accept these migrant groups with their different languages and ways of life, feeling that they are taking jobs and housing from British-born people. There have been considerable social tensions just as there were when the Irish and Russian immigrants arrived in the previous century.

▼ Pedestrians crossing a London street in 2015

10. Society and family

Changes in education meant that far more people went to university. This could lead to a good career but the poorer and least well-educated young men found it hard to get jobs. In 1900, there were millions of jobs in Britain for unskilled men. By 2000, most of these had disappeared as machines could do the work or the industries had died away.

Women had very limited rights in 1900 but it gradually became accepted that they could build their own careers and did not need to stay at home looking after their children. They won equal employment rights and took on jobs that had once been done only by men.

As the authority of the Church declined and fewer people accepted strict religious teaching, divorce became more common. Fewer couples even got married and it became perfectly acceptable to live together and raise children without being married. In many cases, these relationships lasted perfectly well but statistics showed that there were far more single parent families in the last part of the twentieth century. At that time, same-sex relationships became more accepted.

◀ An army dog handler and her dog in the twenty-first century

81

Record

Start making notes in your 'optimist/pessimist' table as explained on page 77.

Reflect

If there are so many problems in gathering reliable statistics about the crime rate, why do you think governments bother to do it?

 # Crime and criminals

As you know by now, statistics about crime can be misleading. From 1898, the government summarised each year's pattern of crime using records kept by police forces and law courts. This certainly helps historians to get a better sense of how patterns of crime were changing over time, but the usual sorts of problem remain, as this table shows:

Problems with crime statistics	Example
Some crimes were not reported to police	Before about 1980, parents, members of the public and even police constables used to punish young troublemakers with a 'clip around the ear' and did not take the matter any further.
Some crimes were reported more than in the past	The number of reported burglaries rose rapidly when insurance companies refused to pay victims if the police had not been informed.
Some offences were no longer crimes	Changes in the law in the 1960s meant that suicide (1961), abortion (1967) and homosexual acts (1967) were no longer crimes.
Some new crimes have been created	Smoking in enclosed public spaces (2007) and in cars with young children (2015) is illegal.
The systems for recording crime change	Significant changes to the way police record crimes were made in 1998 and in 2002. This is why the graph on this page stops in 1998.

From 1900 to 1955

The records show that for the first quarter of the twentieth century, crime continued much as it had before 1900. In the late 1920s and throughout the 1930s, Britain faced severe economic problems and crime began to rise. The police also had to deal with strikes and public protests.

In 1939, when the Second World War started, crime dropped. The following year it rose steeply again. During the Blitz in 1940–41, German aircraft rained bombs on London. The public sheltered in cellars, air raid shelters and the underground. Meanwhile, criminals took to the streets and looted houses and even robbed bodies of jewellery and cash. The stolen goods were often sold on the black market during the war and in the years between 1945 and 1954 while rationing continued. As society settled back to normal life, people probably expected the crime wave to subside. It did not.

Despite all the difficulties with crime statistics, the graph shown here has a pattern that cannot be ignored. There was a significant change around 1955. Even if the graph showed only violent crime it would follow a very similar pattern. If it only showed murders, the line on the graph would fall, but that is largely explained by improvements in medicine: victims who would have died years ago are now kept alive by modern drugs and surgery.

The next three pages will focus on five particular types of crime that worried people after 1955.

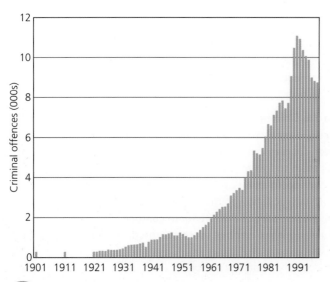

◀ Recorded criminal offences per 100,000 people in England and Wales in the twentieth century

From 1955 to the present

As you study these five different types of crime you will get a sense of how society and crime changed after 1955.

Car crime

On 28 January 1896, Mr Walter Arnold of East Peckham in Kent was the first person in Britain to be caught for speeding in a motor car. A limit of 14 miles per hour (mph) had been set by Parliament the previous year, with a lower limit of 2 mph in towns. Mr Arnold had raced past a policeman in a built up area at about 8 mph. The policeman leapt onto his bicycle and overtook Mr Arnold, charging him with his offence. Car crime in Britain was officially under way.

Over the century speed limits were adjusted but new laws were also passed that caught out many motorists:

- 1967 – A limit was placed on the amount of alcohol allowed in a driver's bloodstream. Police could stop motorists for 'breathalyser' tests to see if they were over the limit.
- 1983 – Drivers had to wear seat belts. By 1991 it was also compulsory for all passengers to wear them.
- 1992 – Fixed roadside cameras captured images of cars that exceeded the speed limit. Guilty drivers had to pay a fine or some might be offered speed awareness training.

Road deaths in Britain have fallen steadily since the 1960s, despite there being far more motorists.

Cars were often stolen. Youths might take a vehicle for a 'joy-ride' and abandon it. Other criminals stole cars, had them re-sprayed and sold them on. Since the 1990s, car locks have improved and thefts have reduced.

▲ A twenty-first century road accident

> ## Reflect
>
> Apart from the laws shown here, what else may have helped to lower the death toll on Britain's roads since the 1960s?

Football hooliganism

Ever since the Middle Ages, football has been associated with crowd violence. The problem reached a peak in the 1970s and 1980s. In 1984, Liverpool fans rioted at a European cup final match at the Heysel stadium in Belgium. In the chaos, a wall collapsed and 39 people died. That led to big changes in security at matches. Since the late 1980s, police have used closed-circuit television to identify dangerous fans. Leading grounds are equipped with seats so that crowd numbers are controlled and fan movement is limited. Football is so popular that ticket prices have soared. Fans mainly come from wealthier backgrounds and are less likely to be looking to fight. Football-related violence does still happen but it usually takes place away from the stadium at pubs or motorway service stations where rival groups confront each other.

▶ Football hooligans at a match between Birmingham and Leeds in 1985

▲ Doreen Lawrence with a picture of her son Stephen, 2006

Race, religion and hate crimes

The immigrants who came to Britain from Commonwealth countries after the Second World War often met with an unpleasant response. Like the Irish and Russians of the nineteenth century, they were given the worst places to live and the lowest paid jobs. There had been communities of black African or Asian origin in Britain for hundreds of years but they had grown slowly over time. The sudden arrival of thousands of Commonwealth citizens came as a shock to many British people whose response ranged from cold indifference to physical violence.

From the 1960s, governments passed laws to try to ensure all British citizens had equal rights, regardless of the colour of their skin. Race Relation Acts were passed in 1965, 1968 and 1976. These made it a crime to deny black people jobs or access to places such hotels or cinemas on account of their colour. They also made it a crime to encourage racial hatred.

Passing laws does not necessarily change behaviour. Discrimination against black people continued. In 1978, a Bangladeshi garment worker called Altab Ali, was brutally murdered in east London by three white teenage boys. There was outrage for a while but it died down. The case that really changed Britain's approach to race-related crime came fifteen years later.

On 22 April 1993, a nineteen-year-old black man called Stephen Lawrence was stabbed to death while waiting for a bus at Eltham in south-east London. The killers were two white men from the area but it took another nineteen years before they were found guilty of the crime. The fact that they were ever brought to justice owed much to Stephen's parents, especially his mother Doreen Lawrence. She defiantly overcame prejudice in the police force and weaknesses in the law to ensure that her son's killers did not go free. The Stephen Lawrence case led to changes in the law.

- In 2005, Parliament passed a law saying that, for the first time in over eight centuries, someone could be tried for the same offence twice if compelling new evidence came to light.
- In 1998 and in 2003, Parliament created a new category of offence known as 'hate crimes'. Victims or witnesses had to say if they felt that a murder or other serious offence had been committed out of hatred for the victim based on his race, religion, sexual orientation, disability or transgender identity. If the court decided that a crime had been motivated in this way, the judge had to make the sentence even more severe.

Only about 1 per cent of offences are found to be 'hate crimes' but the number has been rising steadily. Some say that this shows that Britain is an increasingly violent society. Others are more optimistic. They say that the figures just reveal hatred that had gone unrecorded in the past and that it is a healthy sign that more victims feel confident enough to bring the hatred into the open in court.

Reflect

Which do you think was the more important change, the Race Relations Acts from 1965 to 1976 or the hate crimes laws of 1998 and 2003?

Illegal drugs

In the early years of the First World War, friends and family could buy packs of cocaine to send to soldiers serving overseas. The army reported this was causing problems so the government banned its use by soldiers in 1916. It remained legal for civilians until 1920, when opium and cocaine became controlled substances, only to be used on doctors' orders.

Britain's serious problems with illegal drug use started in the 1960s. By then, drug taking was on the rise and was closely associated with popular music. Young people in particular found excitement in taking substances that offered short-term pleasure even at the risk of long-term harm to health.

In 1971, Parliament tried to end the growing drug culture by imposing a sweeping ban with severe punishments. It listed illegal drugs in categories A, B and C. Class A drugs carried the most serious punishments. At first anyone guilty of supplying others with Class A drugs would go to prison for 14 years. In 1985, this became a life sentence. But drug smuggling and drug use continued to grow.

Addicts often resort to stealing to buy their drugs but organised crime groups make billions of pounds from smuggling and distributing illegal substances. Gangs in cities and, more recently, in rural areas sell drugs to addicts. Like the young gunman who shot Rhys Jones (see page 77), they will try to kill any rivals.

Governments regularly seek new methods of winning what is sometimes called a 'war on drugs', but none seem to work. They also struggle to keep up with the invention of new chemical mixtures that are initially classified as 'legal highs'. As soon as one of these is banned, a new drug appears.

It can cost you your family.

It can cost you your looks.

It can cost you your health.

It can cost you your possessions.

It can cost you your mates.

It's not long before heroin costs you far more than just money. So even if a friend offers you some for nothing, tell them the cost is too high.

HEROIN SCREWS YOU UP

◀ Anti-drugs poster, 1986

Reflect

How similar is the problem of illegal drugs to the 'gin craze' of the eighteenth century?

Cyber crime

The emergence of the internet in the 1990s turned many otherwise honest citizens into criminals, as downloading films and music from illegal websites did not seem like shoplifting.

The thieves, burglars and robbers of earlier ages all needed to lay their hands on the actual property that they wanted to take. With the arrival of online trade and banking, criminals could steal through 'phishing' emails that tricked people into sharing credit card details or through viruses that detect passwords on personal computers.

The cyber criminals operate on a grand scale too. They hack into the computers of big businesses and government departments, threatening to crash the whole system if they are not paid large sums of money. Or they interfere with a bank's computers and pay money into their own account. Some even wreck systems simply to prove that it can be done and for the pleasure of watching the impact of their crime. The makers of computer security software do all they can to keep their customers' data secure, but they are always behind the hackers.

In 2015, when cyber crime was included in Britain's national crime statistics for the first time, the crime rate more than doubled on the previous year's figures. Some say this explains why the crime rate had seemed to be falling in recent years: criminals were moving away from traditional forms of crime and were moving into cyber crime. The figures from 2015 onwards will always include online fraud and theft.

▲ An online credit card purchase, c.2010

Record

Finish this section's notes in your 'optimist/pessimist' table as explained on page 77.

Enforcing the law 1900 to the present

Record

Continue making notes in your 'optimist/pessimist' table as explained on page 77.

Developments in the police force

In 1908, the Times newspaper proudly boasted that:

> In many a back street and slum [the policeman] is the best friend of a great mass of people who have no other counsellor or protector.

The situation was not really as positive as this. Many of the poor still saw the bobby on the beat as an intruder in their area. But overall the first fifty or sixty years of the twentieth century are often called the 'golden age' of policing. The people's trust and respect for their police was captured in a television drama series called 'Dixon of Dock Green'. This ran from 1955 to 1976 and its success was built on the strong, warm and wise character of Police Sergeant George Dixon.

In the years after 1970, that respect was eroded and in 2005, only 58 per cent of the population said they trusted the police to tell the truth. In 2012, the most popular BBC police drama was 'Line of Duty'. It told the story of deception and corruption within the police force. The public now feels more distanced from the police than in the past. Some say this is largely caused by:

- **Police cars** – Far fewer police officers walk the streets today. Many are in patrol cars as they have far larger areas to cover than in the past. Research shows that bobbies on the beat are popular but they do little to deter criminals.
- **Traffic offences** – Otherwise law-abiding citizens resent being caught speeding or using mobile phones when they are driving.
- **Crowd control** – The police sometimes have to deal with enormous crowds. When all goes well their presence is hardly noticed but at events like the miners' strikes of the 1980s and the protests at the G20 meeting of world leaders in London in 2009, television pictures showed the police using extreme and apparently unnecessary force.
- **Corruption** – In the 1980s a report showed serious corruption in the West Midlands Serious Crime squad. In 2014, West Yorkshire police admitted covering up their mistakes at the 1989 Hillsborough football disaster.

Quite apart from its changing reputation, there have been important developments in the police force since 1900. The boxes on the right will help you to identify some of these.

▲ A bobby on the beat in London, 1900

Organisation

In 1900, there were about 200 separate police forces in Britain each dating back to medieval times when local areas had to organise their own constables.

In 1964, an Act of Parliament reduced this local control. It merged many borough forces with those of the counties so there are now only 43, in England and Wales. The 43 forces are still accountable to local bodies but they work closely together.

Since 2013, Scotland has just one national police force. Some people think it would be better to have a single national police force for England and Wales, but others fear that this would place too much power in the hands of central government.

Reflect

1. How do the two photographs on these pages help to sum up changes in policing since 1900?
2. What do you think Britain can be proud of in her modern police force?

▲ A British police officer in riot gear, 2011

Specialisation

Since 1900, the police have had to become expert at a wide range of activities including:

- predicting, preventing and investigating terrorist attacks
- investigating very complex 'white collar' fraud by big businesses such as banks
- crowd and riot control
- forensic science
- use of firearms.

Community policing

From medieval times, British policing has always been based on the consent of local people. The modern force tries to keep this alive by visiting local schools and encouraging the Neighbourhood Watch scheme, rather like a modern version of the medieval hue and cry. Some communities now doubt the effectiveness of the police and pay for private security firms to patrol their area.

Community support can be lost entirely. Reports by Lord Scarman (1981) into a serious riot in Brixton and by Sir William Macpherson (1999) into the police's handling of the Stephen Lawrence murder case both severely criticised the Metropolitan Police for losing the trust of the black community.

Use of weapons

From 1900 to 2000, British police on the beat never carried firearms. Since then some officers patrolling estates with serious gun problems have been armed but it remains very rare.

Truncheons have been used since the nineteenth century but officers now may use pepper sprays or tasers.

Only about 5 per cent of all police officers are qualified to use firearms. They are usually called out only in emergencies.

Some say British police should be armed just like almost every other force in the world. The police still fear that this would make them too much like an army rather than the servants of the local people.

Recruitment, training and pay

In 1900, police officers were all men from a working-class background with limited education. By 2000, recruits could be male or female and needed to have a good education.

There were 226 women officers in 1939 and 37,000 in 2008. Today, only 4 per cent of police officers are from ethnic minority groups.

In 1900, officers received little or no training. In 1947, a National Police Training College was set up. It provides appropriate starter training for all recruits and allows graduates to move quickly to the level of police inspector.

In 1918–19, police officers went on strike for better pay. It was granted but the police gave up their right to strike. Police pay has been kept at a generally good level since then.

Range of work

As *The Times* newspaper suggested (see page 86), police officers in the 1900s did far more than try to catch criminals. They were also 'counsellors', advising, supporting and offering practical help to people in difficulty.

That range of work continues. A police survey in 1993 calculated that only 18 per cent of calls to the police were crime related. Investigating crime takes up about 30 per cent of police time. The rest of the time might be spent educating the public, planning new strategies, helping people who are locked out of their houses or even delivering babies.

Modern police officers have to spend much more of their time writing up reports on each incident they attend to.

New technology

The enormous advances in technology since 1900 have been used by the police in three way ways. These are shown below.

Identification of criminals

In 1901, it was discovered that there are different types of blood group. The police were soon using this to help identify violent criminals whose clothing carried traces of their victims' blood.

In 1902, fingerprints were first used in a British court. A burglar who broke into a London house left marks on the windowsill. He was a regular thief and the police already had copies of his fingerprints. The match was made and the burglar became the first of many to be found guilty by this technology.

The biggest technological breakthrough of all came in 1984 when Alec Jeffreys, a scientist at the University of Leicester, discovered that each person's DNA is unique. We all leave traces of our DNA wherever we go in hairs or flakes of skin, for example. Professor Jeffreys used his discovery to prove that the man who murdered two young women was not the prime suspect, a seventeen-year-old youth with learning difficulties. It was a twenty-seven-year-old man who worked in a Leicestershire bakery. Ever since then, DNA fingerprinting, as it is called, has been used in thousands of cases. It provided the new evidence that was used to jail the two men who killed Stephen Lawrence (see page 84).

DNA is not faultless, however. In some cases, poorly stored DNA samples have been contaminated and court cases have collapsed as the police evidence has been found to be unreliable.

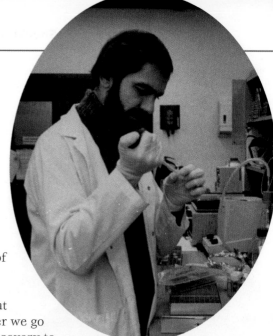

▲ Alec Jeffreys working in his laboratory, 1987

(see page 84)

Reflect

Which of the technological advances mentioned on this page do you think is most important in improving the effectiveness of the police?

▼ A police drone: twenty-first century police surveillance

Communication and data storage

Police forces have always tried to adopt new communication systems quickly and efficiently. Police telephone boxes were first set up in Glasgow in 1891 and the famous blue boxes in London appeared in 1929. Rather than just blow on a whistle, constables could now call for help by telephone. Radio systems were installed in patrol cars in the mid-1960s and portable radios were first used in 1969. These will soon be replaced by a modified mobile telephone system. Some people fear that this will be unreliable and lead to chaos.

DNA tests, fingerprinting and crime reports would be of limited use without the astonishing ability of computers to store and share data of all kinds. Using digital technology, police officers at the scene of a motor vehicle incident can quickly check a driver's registration plates and be notified if he or she has a criminal record.

Surveillance

British police rely heavily on closed-circuit television (CCTV). Cameras in streets record the movements of traffic and pedestrians. Cameras on drones monitor crowds. Some police officers now wear cameras on their uniforms so that their accounts of the incidents they attend can be verified by video.

Surveillance is not only carried out by cameras. In 2015, it was disclosed that police made over 700,000 requests to monitor emails, text messages and internet searches of members of the public. Only about fifty thousand of these requests were denied.

The courts

There were also important changes in the court system in the twentieth century.

The end of local courts

The Courts Act of 1971 swept away the assizes, the quarter sessions and other ancient local courts that had been operating since the Middle Ages. It replaced them all with a new Crown Court. In theory, this is a single court but it sits in over ninety locations around the country and these are often called crown courts. Judges now heard the most serious criminal cases in these courts while magistrates continued to hear less serious cases criminal cases in what were naturally called magistrates' courts. The workings of all these courts are organised by the government under the Ministry of Justice. This is the natural consequence of the gradual move, over several centuries, away from local courts to a national system covering England and Wales. There are, however, different systems in Scotland and Northern Ireland.

Women's roles

After a historic breakthrough in 1918, some British women were allowed to vote in elections. This led to the passing in 1919 of the Sex Disqualification (Removal) Act that opened the way for women to be involved in aspects of society that had until then been denied to them. In 1919, women took their place in juries. Then, in 1920, Ada Summers in Stalybridge, near Manchester, became the first ever woman JP, or magistrate, as they were now called. Today, women outnumber men as magistrates. The work is still unpaid except for a few posts in large cities.

Juvenile courts

By the early twentieth century, psychologists had persuaded many politicians that the best way to improve society was to improve care for children and young people. This led to important changes in maternity support and schools but it also led to the introduction, in 1908, of special juvenile courts where children between the ages of seven and sixteen were to be tried.

A magistrate's court, c.2013. No cameras are allowed in court but there are still seats for members of the public

Juries

Since 1974, there has been no property restriction on who can sit on a jury. This means that juries now reflect the full range of wealth and education in British society. In recent years, governments have tried to reduce the number of trials by jury as they tend to be slow and expensive. The internet is also a problem in jury cases as it is becoming more common for jurors to investigate the case for themselves online. If any member of the jury is found to have done this, the whole case has to start again.

The Crown Prosecution Service

The police took on the responsibility for bringing trials to court during the nineteenth century but in 1986 that role was taken on by the Crown Prosecution Service. It weighs up the police's evidence to decide if there is a strong enough case to put before a court. If it thinks there is enough evidence, it then prosecutes the case either in a magistrates' court or a crown court.

Reflect

What signs can you see in these changes that the running of courts in England and Wales is becoming more centralised?

Record

Finish this section's notes in your 'optimist/pessimist' table as explained on page 77.

As you know, imprisonment became the main form of punishment for criminals during the nineteenth century. Alongside this, corporal punishment continued in the form of whipping with the birch. Hanging was still used for murder and treason. These were deliberately harsh punishments, inflicted in the belief that criminals deserved to suffer and would be deterred from future crime by the fear of future misery.

The last years of the nineteenth century saw a change of approach. Between 1900 and 1970, ideas about the purpose and nature of punishment favoured a more liberal and less harsh approach. Since 1970, the pattern has been less clear.

Corporal punishment

Whipping had been used as a punishment in Britain for centuries. This was often done by a birch, especially for young criminals. By 1900, special wooden restraining benches, like the one shown here, were used to hold the offender in place while he or she was lashed across the back or the buttocks. You can see the birch lying on the top of the block. Although it is called a rod, the birch is made up of several thin supple strands.

In November 1898, a surprised father found his eleven-year-old son with some silver spoons. It turned out that the son and two older boys had stolen them from a local chapel. The father handed his son in to the police and the case went to court. Here is what happened:

▲ A nineteenth-century birching bench

> **21 November 1898 at the Old Bailey, London**
>
> Charles Beckford (11), James Jeffery (13) and James Bryson (13) – Charged with breaking and entering a chapel and stealing eighteen tea-spoons and other articles, the property of Henry Barcham and others. VERDICT: GUILTY. Recommended to mercy by the jury on account of their youth. One day's imprisonment each – Beckford to receive five strokes and Jeffery and Bryson eight strokes each, with a birch rod.

Young Charles Beckford was quite fortunate to get away with only five strokes of the birch. At the time of his offence, a lot of people were putting pressure on the government to make more crimes punishable by a beating rather than a prison sentence. They argued that a beating was quick and cheap and would be an effective deterrent. Surprisingly, perhaps, many liberal-minded people also wanted to use beatings more because they deeply objected to the long drawn-out brutality of a prison sentence.

Others campaigned for an end to all beatings. In time they got their way.

- In 1933, corporal punishment was ended for young offenders.
- In 1948, it was ended as a punishment for all offenders.
- In 1962, it was ended as a punishment for prisoners who misbehaved while locked away.

There have been no serious attempts to bring back corporal punishment for criminals since it was abolished.

Record

Continue making notes in your 'optimist/pessimist' table as explained on page 77.

Reflect

1. Why do you think the judge gave the three boys one day's imprisonment as well as the birching?
2. Why did some liberals suggest that the state might use whipping?

Capital punishment

At eight o'clock in the morning on Thursday 13 August 1964, in a precisely timed operation, two murderers were hanged in two different prisons in Liverpool and Manchester. The men were Peter Allen and Gwynne Evans.

These were the last criminals to be executed in Britain. In 1965, Parliament passed the Abolition of the Death Penalty Act. Although this Act kept capital punishment for offences such as treason, it was never needed after that date. In 2004, all forms of capital punishment for all types of crime were finally and officially abolished throughout the United Kingdom.

The move to abolish capital punishment involved many stages.

▲ Walton prison, Liverpool, 1958. This is where Peter Allen was executed in 1964

Landmarks on the road to the abolition of the death penalty	
1892	The government agreed a standard and efficient method of hanging and trained hangmen in their duties.
1908	No one under the age of sixteen could be executed.
1928	After a debate, Parliament rejected abolition.
1947	The House of Commons voted for abolition but the House of Lords refused to agree.
1953	There was public outcry at the hanging of nineteen-year-old Derek Bentley who had a mental age of ten.
1956	The House of Commons voted for abolition but, once again, the House of Lords refused to agree.
1957	Parliament ended capital punishment for all murders except where a police officer was the victim, a gun was used or the person was resisting arrest.
1965	Parliament passed the Abolition of the Death Penalty Act but only for up to five years to test its effects.
1969	Parliament permanently abolished the death penalty for all murders.

> **Reflect**
>
> Which three events in this landmark list do you think were the most important in ending capital punishment?

When particularly grim murders hit the media headlines, the debate over captial punishment is often revived. People on both sides put forward strongly felt arguments such as these:

Arguments used for capital punishment

- Hanging is a powerful deterrent against murder.
- Murderers should not live in comfort in prison while the family of their victim suffers.
- The British justice systems can be trusted – mistakes are very rare.

Arguments used against capital punishment

- Most murders are done in the heat of the moment with no thought of any deterrents.
- If the state kills people it lowers itself to the level of a murderer.
- Since 1969, over fifty prisoners found guilty of murder have proved their innocence.

In 2012, an online petition calling for the return of the death penalty received over 26,000 signatures, but a counter-petition had over 33,000 supporters. In surveys, though, over 60 per cent of the British public say they want hanging to be re-introduced. Most MPs feel very differently, so there seems to be no chance of Parliament reversing its 1969 decision.

At Wandsworth prison in London, a working gallows was kept ready for use and was tested regularly until 1992. In 1994, it was taken down and moved to a tourist attraction in Nottingham called the Galleries of Justice. Capital punishment in Britain had become a museum piece.

Prisons

This image appeared in 1907 in a magazine published in Paris. The city was experiencing the same sort of gang violence that you read about on page 76. Many people in France believed that their own prison system was too soft. This picture was used in an article describing how British prisons treated their criminals and demanding that similar methods be adopted in France.

The men at the top of the picture are mindlessly walking on a treadmill. It goes nowhere and achieves nothing except to put the men through what was called 'hard labour'. This was supposed to be good for the soul and a strong reason for never returning to prison.

The lower half of the picture shows a prisoner receiving lashes from a whip called the cat o' nine tails. Nine leather thongs tear into the flesh to give a punishment no one would forget. This prisoner is receiving this whipping either as part of his sentence or because he has misbehaved while in prison.

What the French magazine did not understand was that British prisons were turning away from such harsh treatment. The use of treadmills had already been abolished in 1902, five years before this article was published. Other changes followed throughout the century.

▲ A British prison as shown in a French magazine, 1907

Imprisonment of young offenders

By 1900, psychologists and Christian reformers had convinced the government that improved treatment of young people was the key to improving society as a whole. This led to several important changes.

- From 1902 young offenders under the age of 21 went to their own type of prison. The first one opened at a village called Borstal in Kent so later ones all became known as 'borstals'. They were by no means soft on offenders but they tried to educate the inmates and train them in skills that might lead to employment. In 1988, borstals were replaced by young offender institutions. The age range of inmates is usually 18 to 20. Education is still a very important part of the system. Offenders aged between 10 and 17 are now kept in secure children's homes where they, too, receive education and support.
- In 1908, Parliament set down the age at which a child could be held responsible for committing a crime. They set this age of criminal responsibility at seven. It has been adjusted over the years and now stands at ten.

People disagree about how strict juvenile imprisonment should be. Some have favoured what is often called a 'short, sharp, shock'. This means that the institution is deliberately tough. The theory is that a few weeks of this treatment will be enough to stop the young person from offending again. The approach was tried between 1979 and 1990 but there was no clear sign that it was stopping young people from re-offending. Since then the approach has generally been to try to educate young criminals rather than merely punish them.

Reflect

Look back at page 25 where there is a list of issues to consider when deciding how to punish criminals.

Do all those same issues apply when punishing young offenders?

Prison reform

It was not just young offenders who were affected by the reforming work that began around 1900. In 1896, a separate prison called Broadmoor Hospital was set up for those prisoners who were mentally ill. Mainstream prisons for adults also changed, beginning with the abolition of the treadmill in 1902.

The man behind many of the most important prison reforms between 1922 and 1947 was Alexander Paterson. He was a highly educated man and a convinced Christian. He lived for several years in the roughest areas of east London, running a boys' club and getting to know their world. He was put in charge of England's prisons in 1922.

Paterson wanted to turn prisons into places where criminals were rehabilitated and left with the desire and ability to live an honest life. He believed that the only real deterrent was the certainty of being caught. He also once said that people 'are sent to prison as a punishment, not for punishment'. This view shaped many of the changes that he made:

▲ Sir Alexander Paterson, 1939

- The rule that prisoners should stay silent was greatly relaxed.
- Prisoners did not have to have their heads shaved.
- The arrows on prisoners' uniforms were removed.
- Educational work in prisons was greatly increased.
- Prisoners did more meaningful work such as making mats.
- Prisoners were paid a small sum for the work they did.

Paterson realised that some prisoners could not be rehabilitated. One of his last actions was to include a clause in the Criminal Justice Act of 1948 that said prisoners could be kept in prison even longer than their original sentence if releasing them might endanger society.

Prison problems

This graph shows clearly that Britain's prison population has risen steeply since the mid-1940s and especially since the 1990s. That is when governments decided to try to halt the rise in the crime rate by allowing judges to impose longer sentences. There were other reasons for the population rise:

- Magistrates make more use of short prison sentences. Over 80 per cent of prisoners have sentences of less than one year.
- Some criminals who are given fines cannot pay them and so go to prison after all.
- Courts cannot keep up with their case load and people awaiting trial may spend months in prison.

As numbers rose, the prisons became overcrowded. In 2009, Shrewsbury prison held 316 inmates. It was built for 177. In 1990, overcrowding led to a riot at Strangeways prison in Manchester. It lasted 25 days, caused massive damage and took two lives. Overcrowding may also contribute to other problems: a man in prison is five times more likely to commit suicide than a free man outside.

Governments tried to improve space and conditions by building more than twenty-five new prisons between 1985 and 2006. To cut costs to the taxpayer, since 1992 some low risk prisons have been run by private security firms. The firms are paid a fixed amount for each prisoner and make a profit by keeping costs down. They still have to keep to standards set by the government for all prisons.

> ## Reflect
> What do you think was the point of each of these changes to prisons made by Paterson?

▼ Prison population in England and Wales, 1930 to 2010

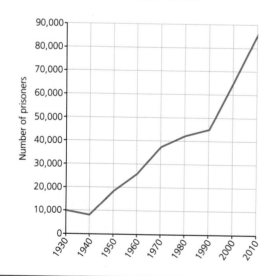

> ## Reflect
> Is it fair to compare private prisons today with the times when gaolers made money from their prisoners in the Middle Ages and the early modern period?

Alternatives to prison

People sometimes wonder whether prison really works. Most prisoners re-offend and return to prison where they learn even more about crime and may become drug addicts. In recent years, prisons have had dreadful problems with drugs that are smuggled in. Drugs and weapons have even been flown in by drones! On top of all this, prisons are extremely expensive. A study in 2007 estimated it cost about £27,000 each year to keep someone in prison.

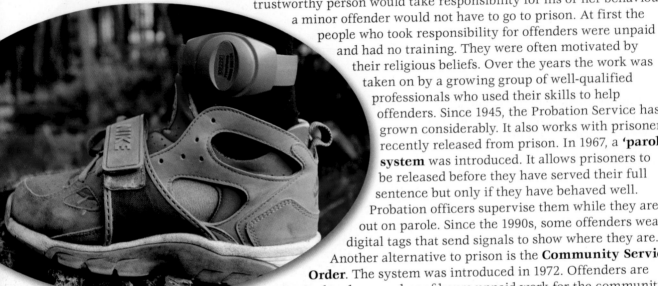

▲ An electronic tag c.1999

In 1907, the government introduced the **Probation Service**. If a trustworthy person would take responsibility for his or her behaviour, a minor offender would not have to go to prison. At first the people who took responsibility for offenders were unpaid and had no training. They were often motivated by their religious beliefs. Over the years the work was taken on by a growing group of well-qualified professionals who used their skills to help offenders. Since 1945, the Probation Service has grown considerably. It also works with prisoners recently released from prison. In 1967, a **'parole' system** was introduced. It allows prisoners to be released before they have served their full sentence but only if they have behaved well. Probation officers supervise them while they are out on parole. Since the 1990s, some offenders wear digital tags that send signals to show where they are. Another alternative to prison is the **Community Service Order**. The system was introduced in 1972. Offenders are required to do a number of hours unpaid work for the community rather than go to prison. The system has developed so that the offender might now do a combination of activities such as:

- unpaid work
- education activities often on literacy or numeracy
- mental health treatment
- drug or alcohol treatment.

Victims

In 1990, the government responded to the public's concerns that criminals were not the only ones who deserved support from the state: so did their victims. It introduced what was then called the Victim's Charter and later became the Victim's Code. It set out the rights of victims and the support they can expect as a criminal case proceeds. One major change was that it gave victims the right to make a Victim's Personal Statement (VPS) explaining how the crime has affected them. They read it aloud to the criminal once a guilty verdict has been reached. Some prefer another person to read it for them.

Two people who never had the chance to make a VPS were 38-year-old Fiona Pilkington and her disabled 18-year-old daughter, Francecca. They were victims of dreadful bullying by youths for over ten years. The police did little or nothing to help and her neighbours failed to realise how desperate Fiona was. In October 2007, Fiona drove Francecca to a layby, poured petrol all over the inside of the car, sat inside with her daughter and lit a match. They burned to death.

It is incidents like this that can make us feel that in the battle against crime, despite all the new approaches, we are getting nowhere.

Reflect

What might be the benefits of a Victim's Personal Statement?

Record

Finish this section's notes in your 'optimist/ pessimist' table as explained on page 77.

▲ The figure of Justice above the Old Bailey, London

Review

You have been gathering evidence from the story of crime and punishment in the twentieth century to help you to decide whether you are optimistic or pessimistic about the future. In this sense, you have been acting like a judge and jury. You have seen the evidence, now you must reach a judgement.

The image above shows the figure of Justice, standing above the court of Old Bailey in London. In her left hand she holds the scales of justice. They symbolise the way courts weigh up the evidence. The sword represents decisive action. You will need both of these concepts as you review what you have learned in the enquiry.

For each of the following issues, use your notes to decide whether you are optimistic or pessimistic about the future of each one. Write a clear explanation that sums up your thinking. Use examples to support your judgement. Do not be indecisive: just like a judge or jury, you must decide one way or another.

- crime and criminals since 1900
- policing and the courts since 1900
- punishment since 1900
- an overall verdict considering all three of the above

When you weigh the evidence, do not just count up which side of the argument has most notes. This is not about quantity, but quality. Which evidence is most convincing and why?

'It took a riot'

▲ Strangeways Prison, Manchester, in April 1990

On Sunday 1 April 1990, the governor of Strangeways prison in Manchester was at home when he received a telephone call. He was told a massive riot had started at the prison and that he needed to get there straight away. His son said it must be an April Fool's day joke. In all senses, it was no joke.

By midday, when the governor arrived, the prison was on fire. Prison officers had managed to secure the exits so no one had escaped, but inside a battle was raging. The prisoners were using table legs, fire buckets and even batteries inside socks as their weapons. They had lit fires and had broken onto the roof. From there they hurled slates down on the prison officers and police in the prison yard below.

The first rioters had taken keys from prison officers and opened cells, releasing fellow prisoners. Many of these had given themselves up straight away and the prison officers had captured many more, but at the peak of the disturbance there were about 700 rioters against about 200 prison officers. The rioters also turned on fellow prisoners in C wing which housed sex offenders. They beat them up and left them to suffer. As the prison officers carried the wounded across the yard to ambulances, rioters on the rooftop urinated on them.

News reports went out saying that the prisoners had raided medicine cabinets and were high on drugs; over twenty people had been killed; sex offenders were being castrated. None of this was true.

It was brutal and violent but there was a point to all this. One rooftop rioter called out to the public and press below: 'We are having no more! We are humans not animals!'

As night fell about 150 rioters were still on the loose and they controlled the upper areas of the prison as well as the roof. Over the next two days more fierce battles took place, but about twenty-five rioters refused to give in. They were determined to make their concerns known to the world. On the roof, in front of the world's cameras, they displayed messages on bed sheets and on a large blackboard moved from a prison classroom. They arranged for a local reporter to come inside and interview them. Their demands became clear:

- They wanted to be allowed to hug their loved ones on visits as any physical contact had been banned.
- They wanted an end to being locked in the cells for over 22 hours a day with just an hour of exercise.
- They wanted an end to 'slopping out'. The lavatories that had been removed from prison cells in the 1860s had never been brought back. The prisoners still had to use a bucket as a toilet, sharing it with one or two others in their small cell. Each morning they had to empty it or 'slop out'.
- They wanted decent food.
- They wanted brutal and racist prison officers to be removed from their jobs.
- They wanted an end to the 'liquid cosh', a powerful sedative that prison officers could inject into any inmate who was resisting them.

Their voice was heard. On 5 April, the government announced that there would be a full enquiry into the riot and its causes. The prisoners held on for another three weeks. The last five left the roof on 25 April.

Two men died in the riot, a prison officer who had a heart attack and a sex offender who was beaten by rioters who were never identified. In two trials, over twenty prisoners were tried and found guilty of various offences. Their sentences were extended by several years each.

There was an enquiry into the riot, led by Lord Woolf. It reported in October 1990 and backed up everything the prisoners had said about conditions in Strangeways. In particular, it criticised the dreadful overcrowding. On the day the riot started there were 1647 prisoners at Strangeways in spaces that were meant to hold 970. The report also demanded that slopping out must be ended and lavatories be built in all prison cells.

The government acted on this and slopping out ended in 1996. There were other improvements in Britain's prisons for several years but, in 2015, on the twenty-fifth anniversary of the riot, Lord Woolf warned that any progress had been lost. There were by then twice as many prisoners in Britain's prisons as there had been in 1990. Overcrowding was back and the pressures were building. Another 'Strangeways riot' could easily happen.

In May 1994, at a cost of over £90 million, a rebuilt and refurbished Strangeways opened in Manchester. As the opening ceremonies took place one prisoner told a visiting journalist:

But for the riot, we would still be in the same old jail banged up all day and slopping out. The rioters brought this about. These improved conditions should not have cost the lives of a prisoner, a prison officer and two huge court trials. They should have done it years ago but it took a riot to get them to do it.

Preparing for the examination

The thematic study forms the first half of Paper 1: British History. It is worth 20 per cent of your GCSE. To succeed in the examination you will need to think clearly about different aspects of crime and punishment and to support your ideas with accurate knowledge. This section suggests some revision strategies and explains the types of examination questions which you can expect.

Period summaries

Your study of Crime and Punishment in Britain has covered four periods of history. You began each period with an overview and made some good guesses about how the characteristic features and major changes of each period might have impacted on crime and punishment. Now you can use your knowledge to produce a detailed and accurate summary for each period. Use the ones we've started to create your own summaries. You might find it helpful to refer to the pictures and text for the overviews on pages 10–13, 32–35, 54–57 and 78–81.

1. Mind map

A mind map on A3 paper is a good way to summarise the important points for a particular period. A mind map will allow you to show connections between different points. It would be a good idea to use different colours for the overview and each of the three main issues.

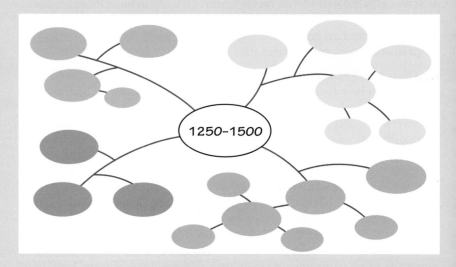

1250–1500

2. Chart

If you find it easier to learn information from lists, then a summary chart for each period might be best for you. You can use the format shown or design you own. Just make sure you include summary points for the overviews and each of the three main issues.

1500–1750	Overview	
	•	
	•	
	•	
Nature and extent of crime	Enforcement of law and order	Punishment of offenders
•	•	•
•	•	•
•	•	•

3. Small cards

Small cards are a flexible way to make revision notes. You could create sets of revision cards for the overview and for each of the three main issues. It would be a good idea to use a different colour for each set of cards.

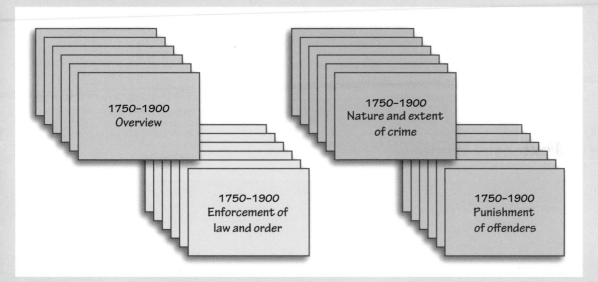

4. Podcasts

If you learn best by listening to information, you could record your knowledge and understanding of a particular period by producing podcasts to summarise the overview and each of the three issues. You could produce your podcast with a friend, using a question and answer format.

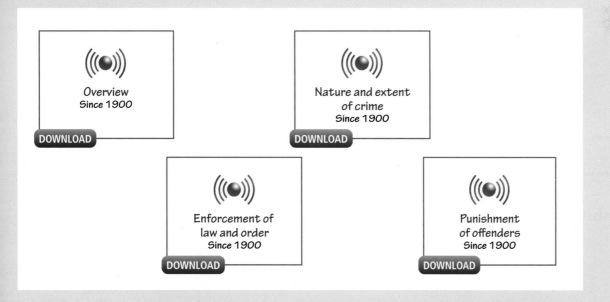

To be well-prepared for the examination you need revision notes which summarise the main points and provide detailed examples in a format that you find works best for you.

Your study of crime and punishment has been organised around three big issues:

- the nature and extent of crime
- the enforcement of law and order
- the punishment of offenders.

Some of the changes and continuities in each of these issues are shown on the timelines below. Use the notes you have made for each enquiry to produce your own detailed summary of the changes and continuities in each issue. You might find it helpful to refer to the pages detailed in the table on the right:

The nature and extent of crime

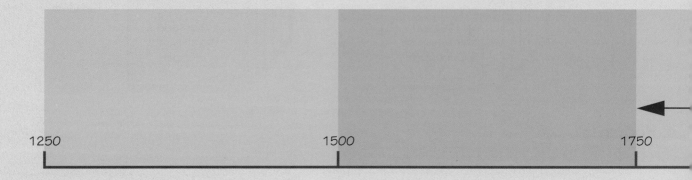

The enforcement of law and order

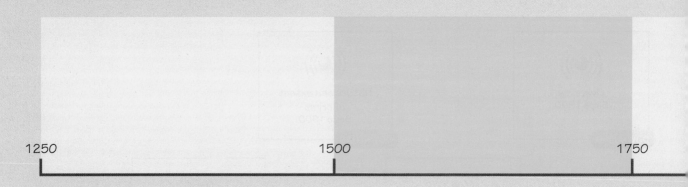

The punishment of offenders

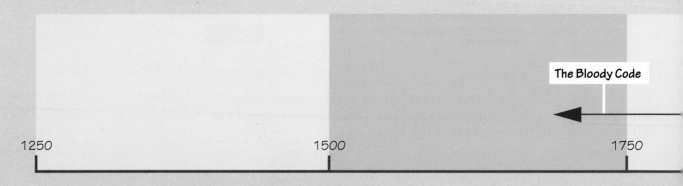

The Bloody Code

	Medieval	Early modern	Industrial	Since 1900
Nature and extent of crime	14–19	36–41	58–61	82–85
Enforcement	20–23	42–45	62–65	86–89
Punishments	24–27	46–49	66–73	90–95

For each issue, use your summaries to identify:

- periods of great change
- specific turning points
- periods of continuity.

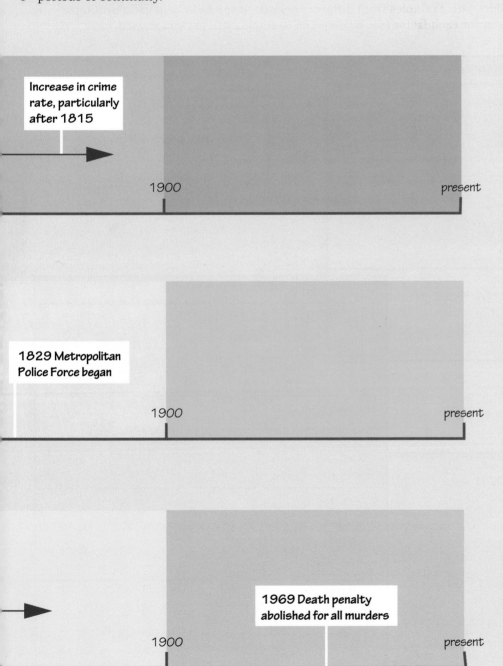

Increase in crime rate, particularly after 1815

1900 · present

1829 Metropolitan Police Force began

1900 · present

1969 Death penalty abolished for all murders

1900 · present

Why things changed or stayed the same

As well as explaining the patterns of change and continuity across time, historians also explain why things change and stay the same. Your study has focused on the ways in which the following five factors influenced changes and continuities in crime and punishment:

1. Beliefs, attitudes and values
2. Government
3. Science and technology
4. Urbanisation
5. Wealth and poverty

Use your notes for Crime and Punishment to create your own factor folders with examples from different periods. It might help to use a different colour for each factor (see below). The examples will get you started.

Beliefs, attitudes and values
1250–1500 Church enforced public humiliation for moral crimes...
1500–1750
1750–1900
Since 1900

Wealth and poverty
1250–1500
1500–1750 Late sixteenth century: rise in food prices caused increase in crime...
1750–1900
Since 1900

Urbanisation
1250–1500
1500–1750
1750–1900 Growth of towns in first half of nineteenth century led to increase in crime...
Since 1900

Government
1250–1500
1500–1750 Government introduced harsh new laws against witchcraft...
1750–1900
Since 1900

Science and technology
1250–1500
1500–1750
1750–1900
Since 1900 Emergence of internet in 1990s led to cyber crime...

Exam guidance

The thematic study forms the first half of Paper 1: British History. It is worth 20 per cent of your GCSE. The whole exam lasts for 1 hour 45 minutes so you will have just over fifty minutes to answer the four questions on Crime and Punishment.

Question 1

You will be asked three quick questions each worth one mark. Question 1 requires you to show factual knowledge about Crime and Punishment. The questions will usually begin *'Give one example of ...'*, *'Name one ...'*, *'Which ...?'*, *'Name the ...'* or *'What was ...?'*

Example

1 a Name one type of official who was responsible for enforcing law and order in the Middle Ages. (1 mark)
   b Name one type of crime that the authorities were particularly worried about in the period 1500–1750. (1 mark)
   c To which country were convicts transported after 1787? (1 mark)

Make a list of ten questions which you think would make a good Question 1.

Question 2

This question is worth 9 marks. It will always begin 'Write a clear and organised summary that analyses ...'. You might be asked to write a narrative account of how an aspect of Crime and Punishent changed over time or a description of an aspect of Crime and Punishment at a particular time.

Example

2 Write a clear and organised summary that analyses how law and order was enforced in the period 1500–1750. Support your summary with examples.

(9 marks)

Think of five more good questions for the summary task.

Question 3

This is an explanation task worth 10 marks. Typical questions will begin with 'Why ... ?', 'Why did ... ?', 'What was the impact of ... ?', 'What caused ... ?', 'Why do you think ... ?'

Example

3   What caused the increase in crime in the first half of the nineteenth century? Support your answer with examples.   (10 marks)

Think of five more good questions for the explanation task.

Question 4/5

You have a choice of two judgement questions, Question 4 or Question 5. These questions in the first part of Paper 1 are the most challenging because they ask you to make a judgement about an aspect of Crime and Punishment. You need to save enough time for the judgement question because it is worth 18 marks. The question will always ask you 'How far' you agree with a given statement.

Examples

4   How far do you agree that the most important changes in the punishment of offenders took place in the twentieth century? Give reasons for your answer.   (18 marks)

5   'In the period between 1750 and 1900 there were big changes in policing.' How far do you agree with this statement? Give reasons for your answer.   (18 marks)

Think of five more good questions for the judgement task.

Glossary

abolish ban something

Act a new law passed by Parliament

archives historical records and documents

arson deliberately setting fire to a house or other property

Assizes the main courts for dealing with serious crimes until 1971

Bill the name given to an act before it is passed by Parliament

burglary breaking into a house or other property in order to steal things

capital punishment execution of various kinds including, hanging, beheading and burning at the stake

coroner a person who investigates a sudden death

corporal punishment physical punishment such as whipping or birching

constable an official with responsibility for maintaining law and order

Crown Court the court introduced in 1971 to replace the Assizes and the Quarter Sessions

execute put someone to death

factor something that plays a part in causing an event or development

famine when people die due to food shortage

felony a serious crime

fine punishment by paying money

gaol a prison

gentry wealthy people who owned land and were often Justices of the Peace

hate crime crime committed against someone because of their race, religion, sexual orientation, disability or transgender identity

heresy beliefs which are not allowed by the Church

homicide killing another human being

illegitimate someone whose parents were not married to each other

imprisonment punishment by being kept in a prison

industrialisation the development of industry, involving the growth of factories and cities

Justice of the Peace (JP) a person who was responsible for maintaining law and order in a county

larceny theft

manslaughter killing someone accidentally

manor an area of land controlled by a lord

Manor Court the court in a manor which administered the lord's lands, but which also judged petty crimes

medieval from the Middle Ages

moral crime offences which were considered to be sinful

middling sort people in the middle of society, neither rich nor poor

minister either an important politician or a vicar

murder a form of homicide where someone intended to kill another person

mutilation punishment by cutting off parts of the body or branding the skin

outlaw someone who is on the run to escape the law

parish the area served by a church

petty crime a minor crime such as theft or damaging property

pillory a wooden frame used for punishing an offender

plague a disease that first appeared in England at the Black Death in 1348

poaching entering land illegally in order to steal animals

probation system for monitoring offenders introduced in 1907

Protestant a Christian who broke away from the old Roman Catholic Church

Puritan a strict Protestant who wanted people to obey the bible and live pure, holy lives

Quaker member of a Christian Church that has a strong tradition of challenging social injustice

Quarter Sessions the county courts which tried criminals four times a year

radical someone who wants to make big changes

reform change something for the better

Reformation the time in the sixteenth century when many Protestant churches started

rehabilitate help someone to become a law-abiding citizen

retainers soldiers in a private army belonging to a lord

robbery violent theft

sanctuary a custom which protected criminals while they were in the grounds of a church

scolding using offensive or abusive speech

secular non-religious; to do with human affairs without any involvement of God or the church

Sheriff the monarch's chief law-enforcer in each county

smuggling secretly importing goods in order to avoid customs duties

statute a law

stocks wooden blocks used to hold an offender's legs

transportation system for taking prison convicts to spend years away from home in a distant land

treason the crime of plotting against your monarch or country

trial the process used to determine whether a person is innocent or guilty

trial by combat a fight to determine whether someone was innocent or guilty

urban to do with towns or cities

urbanisation the rapid growth of towns and cities

vagrant a person who wandered from place to place in search of work

verdict the decision of a jury

Index

Acknowledgements

The publishers would like to thank the following for permission to reproduce copyright material:

Text acknowledgements: p.36 *l* J.A. Sharpe, Crime in Early Modern England, (Longman 1984).p 58; *r* J.A. Sharpe, Crime in Early Modern England, (Longman 1984).p 64; **p.39** James Sharpe, Instruments of Darkness, Witchcraft in England 1550-1750 (Hamish Hamilton, 1996) p. 109; **p.59** Clive Elmsley, Crime and Society in England, 1750-1900(Longman, 1987) p. 35.

Photo credits: p.6 © The British Library Board/Royal 10 E. IV, f.49v; **p.7** © The British Library Board/Royal 10 E. iv; **p.8** © Lebrecht Music and Arts Photo Library/Alamy; **p.10** © Kevin George/Alamy; **p.11** *t* © Granger, NYC./Alamy; *c* © British Library/Robana/REX/Shutterstock; *b* © Speed, John (1552-1629)/Private Collection/Bridgeman Images; **p.12** *t* © Robin Weaver/Alamy; *c* © British Library, London, UK/Bridgeman Images; *b* © British Library/Robana/REX/Shutterstock; **p.13** *t* © Historic England/Mary Evans; *b* © Bibliothèque nationale de France; **p.16** Add 42130 f.172v Peasants harvesting, begun prior to 1340 for Sir Geoffrey Luttrell (1276-1345), Latin (vellum), English School, (14th century) / British Library, London, UK / © British Library Board. All Rights Reserved / Bridgeman Images); **p.18** *t* © The British Library Board; b © De Agostini/M. Seemuller/Getty Images; **p.19** © The Trustees of the British Museum; **p.20** *t* © Montagu Images/Alamy; *tc* © British Library/Robana/REX/Shutterstock; *c* © World History Archive/Alamy; *bc* © British Library/Science Photo Library; *b* © Print Collector/HIP /TopFoto; **p.21** *t* © World History Archive/Alamy; *c* © TopFoto; *b* © travelibUK/Alamy; **p.22** © Rijksmuseum, Amsterdam; **p.24** *t* © Neil Holmes/Getty Images; *b* © Culture Club/Getty Images; **p.25** © Heritage Image Partnership Ltd/Alamy; **p.26** © Mary Evans Picture Library/Francis Frith; **p.28** © Colin Underhill/Alamy; **p.29** © World History Archive/Alamy; **p.30** © Tatton Park, Cheshire, UK/National Trust Photographic Library/Bridgeman Images; **p.31** © Lebrecht Music and Arts Photo Library/Alamy; **p.32** *t* © The Cheltenham Trust and Cheltenham Borough Council/Bridgeman Images; *b* © Private Collection/Bridgeman Images; **p.33** *t* © Classic Image/Alamy; *c* © Dea Picture Library/Getty Images; *b* © Print Collector/Print Collector/Getty Images; **p.34** *t* © The Art Archive/Alamy; *c* © Premier/Alamy; *b* © Granger, NYC./Alamy; **p.35** *t* © Weesop, John (d. c.1653)/Private Collection/Bridgeman Images; *c* © Tilborgh, Gillis van (1625-78)/Tichborne House, Hampshire, UK/Bridgeman Images; *b* © Titlepage of 'The London News', Communicating the High Counsels of Both Parliaments in England and Scotland (woodcut) (b/w photo), English School, (17th century)/Private Collection/Bridgeman Images; **p.37** © Pictorial Press Ltd/Alamy; **p.38** © Universal History Archive/Getty Images; **p.39** © Time Life Pictures/Getty Images; **p.40** © Morland, George (1763-1804)/Fitzwilliam Museum, University of Cambridge, UK/Bridgeman Images; **p.41** © Frith, William Powell (1819-1909)/Manchester Art Gallery, UK/Bridgeman Images; **p.43** © National Portrait Gallery, London; **p.44** © Courtesy of Dorset History Centre; **p.46** *c* © Fotosearch/Getty Images; *b* © Mary Evans Picture Library/Alamy; **p.47** © Mary Evans Picture Library; **p.48** © FalkensteinFoto / Alamy; **p.49** © Mary Evans Picture Library/Alamy; **p.50-51** © Classic Image/Alamy; **p.52** © The National Archives, ref. PCOM 2/291 (253); **p.54** *t* © Mary Evans Picture Library/Alamy; *b* © Illustrated London News Ltd/Mary Evans; **p.55** *t* © Peter Nahum at The Leicester Galleries, London/Bridgeman Images; *c* Courtesy of Manchester Libraries, Information and Archives, Manchester City Council; *b* © Manchester Art Gallery, UK/Bridgeman Images; **p.56** *t* © TopFoto; *c* © AF Fotografie/Alamy; *b* © Print Collector/GettyImages; **p.57** *t* © TopFoto; *c* © TP Archive/ILN/Mary Evans Picture Library; *b* © Mary Evans Picture Library/Alamy; **p.59** © Guildhall Library & Art Gallery/Heritage Images/Getty Images; **p.60** © Mary Evans Picture Library/Alamy; **p.61** *t* © Courtesy of Dorset History Centre; *b* © John Frost Newspapers/Alamy; **p.62** © Photograph supplied with thanks to liverpoolcitypolice.co.uk; **p.63** *r* © National Portrait Gallery, London; *l* © Chronicle/Alamy; **p.64** *t* © Classic Image/Alamy; *b* © Hulton Archive/Getty Images; **p.65** © Courtesy of Jersey Heritage; **p.66** Newspaper image © The British Library Board. All rights reserved. With thanks to The British Newspaper Archive (www.BritishNewspaperArchive.co.uk); **p.68** © Time Life Pictures/Getty Images; **p.69** Mitchell Library, State Library of New South Wales, digital order no. a1644003; **p.70** © Angelo Hornak/Alamy; **p.71** © Pictorial Press Ltd/Alamy; **p.72** © Chronicle/Alamy; **p.73** *t* © Hulton Archive/Getty Images; *b* © Heritage Image Partnership Ltd/Alamy; **p.74** © Sputnik/Alamy; **p.75** © World History Archive/Alamy; **p.76** © Illustrated London News Ltd/Mary Evans; **p.77** © Dave Kendall/Stringer/Getty Images **p.78** *t* © Deco/Alamy; *b* © By Kind permission of The Spectator 1828 Ltd; **p.79** *t* © Kumar Sriskandan/Alamy; *c* © Science Photo Library/Alamy Stock Photo; *b* © mattphoto/Alamy; **p.80** *t* © Wavebreak Media ltd/Alamy; *c* © Science and Society/Superstock; *b* © Rosie Greenway/Getty Images; **p.81** *t* © Grant Rooney/Alamy; *b* © Dorset Media Service/Alamy; **p.83** *t* © Brendan Bell/Alamy; *b* © Trinity Mirror/Mirrorpix/Alamy; **p.84** © Jeff Overs/Getty Images; **p.85** *t* © Contraband Collection/Alamy; *b* © Anna Berkut/Alamy; **p.86** © Chusseau-Flaviens/George Eastman House/Getty Images; **p.87** © Chris Cooper-Smith /Alamy; **p.88** *t* © Terry Smith/Getty Images; *b* © John Giles/PA Archive/Press Association Images; **p.89** © Loop Images Ltd/Alamy; **p.90** © travelibUK/Alamy; **p.91** © Len Forde/Associated Newspapers/REX/Shutterstock; **p.92** © The Print Collector/Alamy; **p.93** © National Portrait Gallery, London; **p.94** © Gianni Muratore/Alamy; **p.95** © Jonathan Buckmaster/Alamy; **p.96** © John Giles/PA Archive/Press Association Images.